RICO

FRANCIA

S. Sebastián
Bayona
*Tolosa

VIZCAYA

Bilbao
VASCON-
GADAS
ÁLAVA NAVARRA

Logroño

LL A

IEJA Soria

Duero Calatayud

Sigüenza

Guadalajara
Alcalá de
Henares

STILLA

A N A

NUEVA

Alcázar

Argamasilla

Valdepeñas

MURCIA

ÍA

SIERRA NEVADA

Almería

I. ALBORAN
(Esp.)

Melilla

Ebro

Zaragoza

ARAGÓN

Teruel

Cuenca

Turia

Valencia

Jucar

Carcagente
Alcoy Denia

Alicante

Murcia

Lorca

Cartagena

Seo de Urgel
Andorra

Lérida

Reus
Tortosa

CATALUÑA

Sabadell Barcelona

Gerona

Tarragona

GOLFO
DEL
LEÓN

ISLAS BALEARES

MENORCA

Palma
MALLORCA

IBIZA

FORMENTERA

MAR MEDITERRÁNEO

Argel

Orán

ÁFRICA

MANHATTAN DRAFTING CO. INC., N.Y.

Tues. 1st 6 lessons + review
Wed. 6 - 9 - 8
Thur 9 -10 - Review
Fri — 11 - 12 - 13
Sat - 14 - 15 -16

Dec. 17

Thur   1 — PM — to 4 PM

S.S. 100

Postal

Dec 16

Wed   10 — 12   speech

are
Dec 18   7:45 — 9:45

Exer
Dec 17   9:45 = 11:45
Thurs.

Basic Spanish

Cuentos y verso
americanos   Walsh

Mon Aprs 26   1. to 4

           Sae Se. 100

Basic Spanish

Joseph W. Barlow

New York University

F. S. Crofts & Co.

New York · 1942

Preface

Basic Spanish is not a revision of the author's *Fundamentals of Spanish*, but an entirely new book. It represents an attempt to present in twenty-five lessons (1) the constructions of highest frequency, (2) a truly basic vocabulary, and (3) the commonest idioms. The twenty-five lessons and the five **repasos** can be completed by college classes in one semester and by high-school classes in one year. In the preparation of the text, constant use has been made of Keniston's *Spanish Syntax List*, Buchanan's *Graded Spanish Word Book*, and Keniston's *Spanish Idiom List*, each of which has a genuinely scientific basis. None of these lists lays claim to perfection. There is, however, little doubt that the constructions, words, and idioms of highest frequency included in them are those that should be mastered first by one who is beginning the study of Spanish.

CONSTRUCTIONS. The *Spanish Syntax List* clearly demonstrates that a number of constructions, hitherto considered essential, are not of sufficient importance to justify their inclusion in a beginning text. All such constructions have been omitted. On the other hand, a few constructions, hitherto accorded only casual notice or omitted altogether, have been emphasized, since the syntax count shows them to be of prime importance. A conspicuous example is the **como si** clause, or, as Professor Keniston calls it, the clause of "imaginative comparison," found to be one of the commonest constructions with the subjunctive.

VOCABULARY. The words (not including numerals and proper names) used in the illustrative reading material and in the exercises number 545. They were chosen from the Buchanan list as follows: 499 from the first 500 words,[1] 34 from the next 300 words, and 12 (**acostar, adiós,**

---

[1] quienquiera has been excluded, since the author is convinced that it appears erroneously in the list of 189 words omitted from the count.

v

ahí, anoche, ante, café, cuento, inglés, mal *noun,* querido *adjective,*
seguida, automóvil) from beyond the first 800. Not used in the lessons, but included as optional vocabulary, are 113 additional words,
making a total of 658.

OPTIONAL VOCABULARY. Under this heading appear a few common
words and phrases related to the vocabulary of the lesson. They may
be used for additional oral or written work. Optional also are the prov-
erbs and verses.

IDIOMS. The first 34 idioms and 55 others of high frequency from
Part A of Keniston's *Spanish Idiom List* and the phrases of highest
frequency (not classified as idioms) from each of the other categories
are used in the lessons. Other important idioms are listed with the optional vocabulary.

TEXT. Since constructions, idioms, and vocabulary are more readily
learned when presented in a logical sequence of ideas, each lesson begins with a connected text. The greater part of the text matter is dialogue, designed to serve as a basis for conversation, as well as to illustrate all points of grammar.

After the student has acquired some ability to pronounce words and
phrases properly—that is, after the first three or four lessons—he should
be encouraged to read aloud and to try to comprehend the text as he
reads, aided only by the idioms that precede and by the illustrations
and simple explanations of grammatical principles that follow. In other
words, he should avoid the temptation to begin each lesson with a mere
matching of English and Spanish words. Therefore, the text and the
lesson vocabulary do not appear together on the same page. Most students will learn to read in less time and with greater skill if they learn to
read aloud with reasonable correctness of pronunciation and expression.

In an effort to render less troublesome certain difficulties encountered
by all beginning students, great care has been exercised in the order of
presentation of grammatical material. The following examples will
serve to illustrate the point: The verb **estar,** to express location (its
most frequent use), appears in the first four lessons, and with a predicate adjective in Lesson V, before the problem is complicated by the

introduction of **ser**. By deferring the presentation of the present participle until correct habits of expression have been formed, the author has checked the student's tendency to use that participle after prepositions and to use a progressive form where a simple tense is the normal construction. The conventional division into three classes of radical-changing verbs has been discarded. Experience with a preliminary edition of this text seems fully to justify the simpler treatment employed. Object pronouns are introduced gradually, and no involved constructions are used.

APPENDIX. A reasonably complete treatment of verbs will be found in the appendix. The usefulness of this material is not limited to the basic course in Spanish, as the student will find occasion to refer to it in later studies.

SUGGESTIONS. It would be presumptuous to offer experienced teachers detailed suggestions on the most effective manner of using this book. Obviously, the lessons may be treated in a variety of ways. A word may not be amiss, however, concerning one method of presentation that has worked well at New York University.

If the class is not too large, the first three lessons are covered in three periods of one hour each. Thereafter, lessons are divided. The first assignment includes the idioms, the text, and the questions based on the text. In preparation for this assignment, the teacher reads the text (alone, and with the students), not word by word, but in breath groups at normal speed. Each statement of principles is then read aloud, preferably by a student. Brief comment follows if the point is not clearly understood by all. For homework, the student memorizes the idioms and prepares to answer orally, without hesitation, the questions in Exercise A. The writing from dictation of at least a portion of the text frequently forms a part of the following recitation. The second assignment covers the remaining exercises. They provide adequate drill on grammatical principles as well as on forms and vocabulary. Usually a few minutes are devoted to the optional material, especially when common idioms are included.

In high-school classes, where an entire year would be devoted to the mastery of the fundamentals, the lessons can be broken up into as many

assignments as desired. The high-school year of forty weeks provides
two hundred class periods. If an average of five days is devoted to each
lesson and three days to each review, sixty days remain for supplemen-
tary reading and oral work. Upon completion of this course, the stu
dent should be able to read elementary Spanish texts with comparative
ease, even if they have not been greatly simplified.

The author wishes to express to his colleagues at New York University sincere gratitude for using the preliminary edition of this text and
for many helpful suggestions resulting therefrom. To Professor
F. Courtney Tarr of Princeton University he is indebted for a most
painstaking review and detailed criticism of these lessons.

J. W. B.

Contents

Maps

Basic Spanish

Lección Primera

Pronunciation

Your ability to pronounce Spanish words, taken singly and
when linked together in phrases, will depend largely upon your
ability to imitate the pronunciation of your teacher. Since no
letter of the Spanish alphabet is pronounced exactly like the corresponding English letter, it will be understood that the equivalents given in lessons I–III are only approximate. Your teacher
will explain the position of tongue and lips for the production of
each sound.

There is no movement of the tongue during the pronunciation
of a Spanish vowel. The vowel is, therefore, pure, short, and
clear, whether initial, medial, or final. Be careful to avoid the
"glide" with which vowels in English frequently end.

1. Vowels

a, pronounced like *a* in *father*. **la,** *the* **Ana** (A-na), *Anna* **mesa**
(me-sa), *table*

e, pronounced like *e* in *they*, at the end of a syllable.[1] **mesa** (me-sa),
table **de,** *of, from*. Keep the **e** short and clear (no glide).

o, pronounced like *o* in *open*. **lado** (la-do), *side* **come** (co-me), *eats*

i (y), pronounced like *i* in *machine*. **vino** (vi-no), *wine*. The same sound
is represented by **y** when it stands alone or at the end of a word.
y, *and* **muy,** *very*

u, pronounced like *u* in *rule*. **nunca** (nun-ca), *never*

---

[1] Pronounced like *e* in *met* when a consonant ends the syllable. **el,** *the* **pared**
(pa-red), *wall*.

2. Consonants

b and **v** have the same sound. When initial in a breath group or after **m** or **n** (see note 1, p. 11), pronounced like *b* in *boy*. In other positions the lips barely touch. Lower lip must not touch upper teeth. **Venga usted aquí,** *Come here* **también,** *also* **bebe,** *he drinks* **vino,** *wine*

c, pronounced like *c* in *cat*. **carne** (car-ne), *meat* **café** (ca-fé), *coffee*. Before **e** and **i**, **c** is pronounced like *th* in *thin*. **cerca** (cer-ca), *near* **cinco** (cin-co), *five*

d, similar to English *d*, but tongue must touch lower edge of upper front teeth. **dónde** (dón-de), *where*. Between vowels or at the end of a word, pronounced as *th* in *though*. **lado** (la-do), *side* **pared** (pa-red), *wall*

f, l, m, n, p, pronounced about as in English.

qu (**u**, silent), pronounced like *k*. Occurs only with **e** and **i** (**que, qui**). **qué,** *what*

r, pronounced with one flip of tongue against gums of upper front teeth. When initial, it must be trilled. **carne** (car-ne), *meat* **pared** (pa-red), *wall* **Roberto** (Ro-ber-to), *Robert*

s, pronounced like *s* in *see*. **mesa** (me-sa), *table*. Occasionally like *s* in *rose*, especially when it precedes **m** or **d**. **mismo** (mis-mo), *same* **desde** (des-de), *since*

t, similar to English *t*, but tip of tongue must touch inner surface of upper front teeth. **está** (es-tá), *is* **contra** (con-tra), *against*

3. Accent

Rule 1. If the word ends in a consonant (except **n** or **s**), stress the last syllable.

Rule 2. If the word ends in a vowel, **n**, or **s**, stress the next to the last syllable.

Words not pronounced according to the above rules must have a written accent (´).

IDIOMS

al lado de, beside
cerca de, near

---

1. A-na es-tá a la me-sa. 2. ¿Dón-de es-tá la me-sa? 3. La me-sa es-tá cer-ca de la pa-red. 4. El pan es-tá en la me-sa. 5. ¿Dón-de es-tá la car-ne? 6. La car-ne es-tá al la-do del pan. 7. ¿Dón-de es-tá el ca-fé? 8. El ca-fé es-tá cer-ca de la car-ne. 9. ¿Qué co-me A-na? 10. A-na co-me pan y car-ne. 11. ¿Qué be-be A-na? 12. A-na be-be ca-fé. 13. ¿No be-be vi-no? 14. No, A-na nun-ca [1] be-be vi-no.

4. Gender of Nouns

Nouns in Spanish are either masculine or feminine. There are no neuter nouns. Fix in mind the gender of each noun by learning the definite article (**el**, masculine; **la**, feminine) with it.[2]

MASCULINE	FEMININE
el café, *the coffee*	**la carne,** *the meat*
el lado, *the side*	**la mesa,** *the table*
el pan, *the bread*	**la pared,** *the wall*

5. Negative and Interrogative Sentences

The adverb **no,** *no, not,* is placed before the verb to make a sentence negative.

---

[1] If **nunca** follows the verb, no must precede it. **No bebe vino nunca.** *She never drinks wine.*

[2] Nouns ending in -o are generally masculine and those ending in -a are generally feminine. Two important exceptions are **el día,** *the day,* and **la mano,** *the hand.*

   Ana no bebe vino.   *Anna doesn't drink wine.*
   El vino no está en la mesa.   *The wine is not on the table.*

In a question, the subject follows the verb. An inverted interrogation point (¿) is placed before a question.

   ¿Está Ana a la mesa?   *Is Anna at the table?*
   ¿No come Ana la carne?   *Isn't Anna eating the meat?*

6. Contractions

There are only two contractions in written Spanish:

       del (de + el), *of the, from the*
       al (a + el), *at the, to the*

La carne está al lado del pan.   *The meat is beside (at the side of) the*
                               bread.

Exercises

A. *Answer in Spanish with a complete sentence.* 1. ¿Dónde[1] está Ana? 2. ¿Dónde está la mesa? 3. ¿Dónde está el pan? 4. ¿Dónde está la carne? 5. ¿Dónde está el café? 6. ¿Qué come Ana? 7. ¿Qué bebe? 8. ¿Qué no bebe nunca?

B. *Translate orally.* 1. near the wine 2. beside the table 3. on the wall 4. near the bread 5. of the coffee 6. of the meat 7. at the table 8. the coffee and the wine 9. He is eating. 10. Is he drinking?

C. *Translate.* 1. Anna is at the table near the wall. 2. She is eating the bread and drinking the coffee. 3. The bread is beside the meat. 4. The meat is near the coffee. 5. Is the wine near the meat? 6. The wine is not on the table. 7. Doesn't Anna drink wine? 8. No, Anna never drinks wine.

---

[1] The written accent is used to distinguish between two words spelled alike: ¿dónde? ¿qué? (interrogative); **donde, que** (relative). All the interrogatives are accented.

Vocabulary

NOUNS

Ana, Anna
el café, the coffee; the café
la carne, the meat
el lado, the side
la mesa, the table, desk
el pan, the bread
la pared, the wall
el vino, the wine

VERBS

bebe, he (she, it) drinks, is drinking [1]
come, he (she, it) eats, is eating
está, he (she, it) is

ADVERBS

no, no, not
nunca, never

PREPOSITIONS

a, to, at
cerca de, near
de, of, from, with
en, in, on

INTERROGATIVES

¿dónde? where?
¿qué? what?

CONJUNCTION

y, and

OPTIONAL VOCABULARY [2]

el pescado (pes-ca-do), the fish
el plato (pla-to), the plate, dish
la sal, the salt

Refrán (Proverb)

El pan, pan, y el vino, vino.
Plain facts in plain words (To call a spade a spade).

---

[1] The Spanish verb form may be translated in the following ways: bebe, *he drinks, he is drinking, he does drink.* ¿bebe? *is he drinking? does he drink?*

[2] Words given under Optional Vocabulary do not appear in the exercises. They furnish the basis for additional oral drill, when time permits.

Lección Segunda

7. Diphthongs

a, e, o are called strong vowels.
i (y), u are called weak vowels.

Any combination of a strong vowel and a weak vowel forms a diphthong and counts as one syllable. When the weak vowel bears a written accent, the combination forms not a diphthong but two distinct syllables. **María** (Ma-rí-a), *Mary*

ai (ay), pronounced like the English pronoun *I*. **aire** (ai-re), *air*
     hay (h, silent), *there is, there are*
ei (ey), pronounced like *ey* in *they*. **reina** (rei-na), *queen* **rey**, *king*
oi (oy), pronounced about like *oy* in *boy*. **oigo** (oi-go), *I hear* **hoy**, *today*
ia, pronounced like *ya* in *yacht*. **justicia** (jus-ti-cia), *justice*
ie, pronounced like *ye* in *yet*. **también** (tam-bién), *also* **viejo** (vie-jo),
     old
io, pronounced like *yo* in *yoke*. **acción** (ac-ción), *action*

8. Consonants

ch,[1] pronounced like *ch* in *church*. **muchacho** (mu-cha-cho), *boy*
g, pronounced like *g* in *go*. **Gómez** (Gó-mez). Before e and i, this
     sound is spelled **gu** (u, silent). **guerra** (gue-rra), *war*
h, always silent
j, pronounced like *h* in *hawk*. **justicia** (jus-ti-cia), *justice* **hijo** (hi-jo),
     son. Before e and i, this sound is frequently written g. **gente**
     (gen-te), *people* **cogí** (co-gí), *I seized*

---

[1] ch, ll, and rr are considered single consonants. For alphabet and further remarks, see § 134.

6

ll, pronounced like *lli* in *million*, except that **ll** begins the syllable (*mi-llion*). **allí** (a-llí), *there* **caballo** (ca-ba-llo), *horse*

ñ, pronounced like *ny* in *canyon* (Spanish **cañón**). **señor** (se-ñor), *sir*

rr, pronounced with a trill. **r** must also be trilled when initial. **guerra** (gue-rra), *war* **reina** (rei-na), *queen* **rey,** *king*

z, pronounced like *th* in *thin*. **paz,** *peace* **Gómez** (Gó-mez)

IDIOM

hay, there is; there are

---

1. No hay paz en el pa-ís. 2. No, se-ñor, no hay paz. 3. No hay jus-ti-cia. 4. Hay gue-rra. 5. El ge-ne-ral Gó-mez va a la gue-rra. 6. El hi-jo del rey tam-bién va a la gue-rra. 7. ¿Dónde está el hi-jo? 8. Está al lado del ca-ba-llo. 9. Hoy to-ma par-te en la ac-ción. 10. El rey está cerca del ge-ne-ral Gó-mez. 11. El rey no to-ma par-te en la ac-ción. 12. ¿Dónde está la rei-na? 13. La rei-na está cerca del mu-cha-cho. 14. ¿Va el mu-cha-cho a la gue-rra? 15. Sí, se-ñor, el mu-cha-cho va a la gue-rra.

9. Possession

Possession is expressed in Spanish by the preposition **de.**

> **El hijo del rey.** *The king's son.*

10. The Definite Article with Titles

The definite article must be used with a title,[1] except in direct address.

El general Gómez va a la guerra.	*General Gómez is going to the war.*
La señorita Pérez está a la mesa.	*Miss Pérez is at the table.*
But **Señorita Pérez, ¿hay vino en la mesa?**	*Miss Pérez, is there wine on the table?*

---

[1] The titles **don** and **doña,** used with the first name, do not take the article. These titles have no equivalents in English.

Exercises

A. *Answer in Spanish.*[1] 1. ¿Dónde no hay paz? 2. ¿Hay justicia en el país? 3. ¿Qué hay? 4. ¿Adónde va el general Gómez? 5. ¿Adónde va el hijo del rey? 6. ¿Dónde está el hijo del rey? 7. ¿Toma parte en la acción? 8. ¿Dónde está el rey? 9. ¿Toma parte en la acción? 10. ¿Está la reina cerca del rey? 11. ¿Adónde va el muchacho?

B. *Translate.* 1. What is General Gómez eating? 2. He is eating bread and meat. 3. Is there wine on the table? 4. Yes, sir, and there is coffee also. 5. The boy is beside the general. 6. The general takes wine and the boy takes coffee. 7. The king's table is near the wall. 8. The king's son is not at the table today. 9. There is war in the country. 10. The son takes the horse and goes to the war. 11. Is there no peace in the country? 12. No, sir, there is no peace and there is no justice.

Vocabulary

NOUNS

la acción, the action
el caballo, the horse
el general, the general
la guerra, the war
el hijo, the son
la justicia, the justice
el muchacho, the boy
el país, the country
la parte, the part
la paz, the peace
la reina, the queen
el rey, the king

el señor, the gentleman; (*as a title*), Mr., sir

VERBS

hay, there is; there are
toma, he (she, it) takes, is taking
va, he (she, it) goes, is going

ADVERBS

hoy, today
sí, yes
también, also, too

---

[1] Whenever possible, begin your answer with **Sí (No), señor,** *Yes (No), sir,* or **Sí (No), señorita (señora),** *Yes (No), miss (madam).*

INTERROGATIVE	OPTIONAL VOCABULARY
¿adónde? where (*to what place*)?	el palacio (pa-la-cio), the palace
	la princesa (prin-ce-sa), the princess
	el príncipe (prín-ci-pe), the prince

Refrán

A la guerra, con la guerra.
Fight fire with fire.

Lección Tercera

11. Diphthongs

au, pronounced like *ou* in *out*. **autor** (au-tor), *author* **causa** (cau-sa), *cause*

eu (rarely found), pronounced like the combination *e-oo* of *they too*, with the stress on *e*. **Europa** (Eu-ro-pa), *Europe*

ua, pronounced like *wa* in *watt*. **Juan,** *John* **agua** (a-gua), *water*

ue, pronounced like *we* in *web*. **pueblo** (pue-blo), *people, town* **bueno** (bue-no), *good*

uo, pronounced like *wo* in *woke*. **antiguo** (an-ti-guo), *ancient, old*

All the diphthongs studied thus far are combinations of a strong vowel (**a, e, o**) and a weak vowel (**i, u**). Diphthongs are also formed by combining two weak vowels.

iu, pronounced like English *you*, cut short. **ciudad** (ciu-dad), *city*

ui (uy), pronounced like English *we*, cut short. **cuidado** (cui-da-do), *care* **ruido** (rui-do), *noise*

12. Consonants

x, pronounced like *x* in *exact*. **existir** (ex-is-tir), *to exist* Before another consonant, like Spanish *s*. **extraño** (ex-tra-ño), *strange* **explicar** (ex-pli-car), *to explain*

y, pronounced as in English. **y** is a vowel at the end of a word, but it is treated as a consonant in determining the accent (§ 3, rule 1). **ya,** *now, already* **ayer** (a-yer), *yesterday*

IDIOMS

a caballo, on horseback
a pie, on foot
en casa, at home, in the house

— ¿Adónde va usted, Juan?
— Voy a la fuente. No hay agua en casa.
— ¿Dónde está la fuente?
— Está fuera del pueblo.
— ¿Va usted a caballo?
— No, señor, voy a pie. La fuente no está lejos. Está muy cerca.
— ¿Qué libro tiene usted en la mano?
— Tengo una historia de España.
— ¿Vive el autor del libro?
— Sí, señor, el autor vive en un [1] pueblo cerca de la ciudad.

13. Division of Words into Syllables

1. A single consonant (including **ch, ll, rr**) is pronounced with the following vowel: **ge-ne-ral,** *general* **mu-cha-cho,** *boy* **ca-ba-llo,** *horse* **gue-rra,** *war*

2. Combinations of two consonants between vowels are generally separated: **car-ne,** *meat* **nun-ca,** *never* **par-te,** *part*

3. But the combination is generally inseparable if the second consonant is **l** or **r: li-bro,** *book* **pue-blo,** *people, town*

14. Punctuation and Capitalization

1. An inverted interrogation point (¿) and an inverted exclamation point (¡) are placed before a question and an exclamation respectively.

¿**Tiene usted el libro?** *Have you the book?*
¡**Qué muchacho!** *What a boy!*

---

[1] Before a labial consonant (**p, b, v**), **n** is pronounced **m.**

2. The dash (—) is used instead of quotation marks to indicate a change of speakers in a dialogue.

> — ¿Adónde va usted, Juan?
> — Voy a la fuente.

3. Capital letters are not as frequently used in Spanish as in English. Words not capitalized are:

(a) proper adjectives, even when used as nouns:

> el español, *the Spaniard*   el francés, *the Frenchman*

(b) the titles señor, *Mr.*, señora, *Mrs.*, señorita, *Miss*

> La señorita López no está en casa.   *Miss López is not at home.*

(c) days of the week and months of the year:

> lunes, *Monday*   enero, *January*

15. The Subject Pronoun *usted*

Since the ending of the verb form indicates the person, subject pronouns (except **usted**) are usually omitted in Spanish. **usted** (*pl.*, **ustedes**) is used with the third person of the verb. It may be abbreviated to **Vd.** or **Ud.** (*pl.*, **Vds.** or **Uds.**).

tengo,	*I have*	Vd. tiene,	*you have*	tiene,	*he has*
tomo,	*I take*	Vd. toma,	*you take*	toma,	*he takes*
voy,	*I go*	Vd. va,	*you go*	va,	*he goes*

16. The Indefinite Article

The word for *a* or *an* is

> un, before a masculine noun   **un libro,** *a book*
> una, before a feminine noun   **una casa,** *a house*

17. The Definite Article to Express Possession

When referring to parts of the body or to articles of clothing, Spanish generally uses the definite article instead of the possessive adjective.

> ¿Qué tiene Vd. en la mano?   *What have you in your hand?*

Exercises

A. *Answer in Spanish.* 1. ¿Adónde va Juan? 2. ¿Qué no hay en casa de Juan? 3. ¿Dónde está la fuente? 4. ¿Va Juan a caballo a la fuente? 5. ¿Está la fuente lejos del pueblo? 6. ¿Tiene Vd. un libro en la mano? 7. ¿Qué libro tiene Juan? 8. ¿Vive el autor en una ciudad? 9. ¿Dónde está el pueblo? 10. ¿Vive Vd. en un pueblo?

B. *Divide into syllables and underscore the accented syllable.* 1. agua 2. autor 3. casa 4. ciudad 5. España 6. fuente 7. historia 8. mano 9. pueblo 10. usted 11. fuera 12. caballo

C. *Translate.* 1. John lives in a village not far from a city. 2. Do you live in a city too? 3. In John's house there is no water. 4. There is a fountain outside of the town. 5. Are you going to the fountain today? 6. I am not going to the fountain. 7. I am going to the city. 8. I have a book in my hand. 9. On the table there is a history of Spain. 10. The author's house is not far from the city.

Vocabulary

NOUNS

el agua *f.*,[1] the water
el autor, the author
la casa, the house
la ciudad, the city
España, Spain
la fuente, the fountain, spring
la historia, the history, story
Juan, John
el libro, the book
la mano, the hand
el pie, the foot
el pueblo, the town, village

PRONOUN

usted, you

VERBS

tengo, I have
vive, he (she, it) lives, is living
voy, I go, am going

ADVERBS

cerca, near
lejos, far, far away
muy, very

---

[1] agua is feminine (see note 2, p. 3). **el** is used instead of **la** before a noun beginning with a stressed **a-** or **ha-**.

PREPOSITION	OPTIONAL VOCABULARY
fuera de, outside of, out of	**la escuela,** the school; **a la escuela,** to school
	la iglesia, the church; **a la iglesia,** to church

Refrán

Libro cerrado no saca letrado.
A closed book does not produce a learned man.

Lección Cuarta

(FOURTH LESSON)

IDIOMS

ir a casa, to go home
todavía no, not yet

— Estamos en la clase. La clase tiene dos puertas. Tiene cuatro ventanas. En las paredes hay cuadros.

— ¿Hay muchos cuadros?

— No, señor, hay pocos. Hay tres.

— ¿Cuántas mesas hay?

— Hay dos. La mesa del maestro está delante de la clase. Sobre la mesa del maestro hay dos plumas, nueve libros y muchos papeles. La otra mesa está detrás de la clase. Está contra la pared.

— ¿Cuántos muchachos hay en la clase?

— Hay siete muchachos.

— ¿Cuántas muchachas hay?

— Hay ocho muchachas.

— ¿Habla español el maestro?

— Sí, señor, el maestro habla español. También habla francés. Los muchachos hablan inglés.

— ¿No hablan español?

— Todavía no.

18. Plural of Nouns and of the Definite Article

Nouns ending in a vowel add -s to form the plural. Nouns ending in a consonant add -es to form the plural.

The plural of el is los; of la, las.

el cuadro,	*the picture*	los cuadros, *the pictures*
el papel,	*the paper*	los papeles, *the papers*
la puerta,	*the door*	las puertas, *the doors*
la pared,	*the wall*	las paredes, *the walls*

19. Agreement of Adjectives

A Spanish adjective agrees with the noun it modifies in gender (*masculine* or *feminine*) and in number (*singular* or *plural*).

If the masculine singular ends in -o, there are four forms: **otro, otra, otros, otras.**

otro cuadro, *another picture*	otros cuadros, *other pictures*
otra puerta, *another door*	otras puertas, *other doors*

If the adjective does not end in -o, there are two forms: **triste** (*m. & f.*), **tristes** (*m. & f.*).

María está triste.	*Mary is sad.*
Juan y María están tristes.	*John and Mary are sad.*

Adjectives of nationality that do not end in -o add -a to form the feminine. Adjectives of nationality are often used as nouns.

español,	*Spanish (Spaniard)*	española,	*Spanish (Spanish woman)*
francés,	*French (Frenchman)*	francesa,	*French (Frenchwoman)*
mejicano,	*Mexican*	mejicana,	*Mexican*
americano,	*American*	americana,	*American*

20. The Cardinal Numbers

1	uno-a	6	seis
2	dos	7	siete
3	tres	8	ocho
4	cuatro	9	nueve
5	cinco	10	diez

The cardinal numbers from 1 to 100 are invariable, with the exception of **uno -a. uno** drops the **-o** before a masculine noun.

> **un cuadro,** *one picture*
> **una puerta,** *one door*

21. The Verb

Verbs in Spanish are divided into three conjugations, according to the ending of the infinitive: (1) **-ar,** (2) **-er,** (3) **-ir.**

The stem of a verb is found by dropping the infinitive ending:

> **hablar, habl-   comer, com-   vivir, viv-**

Inflectional endings to indicate person, number, and tense are added to the stem.

PRESENT INDICATIVE

First Conjugation		*Second Conjugation*		*Third Conjugation*	
hablar, *to speak*		**comer,** *to eat*		**vivir,** *to live*	
SINGULAR		SINGULAR		SINGULAR	
hablo,	*I speak*	**como,**	*I eat*	**vivo,**	*I live*
hablas	} *you speak*	**comes**	} *you eat*	**vives**	} *you live*
Vd. habla		**Vd. come**		**Vd. vive**	
habla,	*he (she, it) speaks*	**come,**	*he (she, it) eats*	**vive,**	*he (she, it) lives*
PLURAL		PLURAL		PLURAL	
hablamos,	*we speak*	**comemos,**	*we eat*	**vivimos,**	*we live*
habláis	} *you speak*	**coméis**	} *you eat*	**vivís**	} *you live*
Vds. hablan		**Vds. comen**		**Vds. viven**	
hablan,	*they speak*	**comen,**	*they eat*	**viven,**	*they live*

22. Forms of Address

The second person of the Spanish verb (**hablas, comes, vives;** *pl.,* **habláis, coméis, vivís**) may be used only in one's family circle and in speaking to very intimate friends, children, and animals. It is called the "familiar form" of address. For the present, the

student should use only the form with **usted**, already learned
(§ 15).

23. Important Verbs That Must Be Learned Separately

Most verbs follow the models given in § 21, but a number of
very important verbs must be learned separately, because of vari-
ations in stem or endings or both. See § 135.

estar, *to be*		ir, *to go*		tener, *to have* (*possess*)	
estoy,	*I am*	voy,	*I go*	tengo,	*I have*
estás,	*you are*	vas,	*you go*	tienes,	*you have*
está,	*he is*	va,	*he goes*	tiene,	*he has*
estamos,	*we are*	vamos,	*we go*	tenemos,	*we have*
estáis,	*you are*	vais,	*you go*	tenéis,	*you have*
están,	*they are*	van,	*they go*	tienen,	*they have*

Exercises

A. *Answer in Spanish.* 1. ¿Dónde estamos? 2. ¿Cuántas
puertas tiene la clase? 3. ¿Cuántas ventanas tiene? 4. ¿Qué
hay en las paredes? 5. ¿Cuántos cuadros hay? 6. ¿Dónde está
la mesa del maestro? 7. ¿Hay muchas plumas sobre la mesa?
8. ¿Cuántos libros hay sobre la mesa del maestro? 9. ¿Dónde
está la otra mesa? 10. ¿Cuántos muchachos hay en la clase?
11. ¿Cuántas muchachas hay? 12. ¿Hablan francés los muchachos? 13. ¿Qué no hablan todavía? 14. ¿Habla francés en
la clase el maestro?

B. *Translate.* 1. How many feet have you? 2. I have two feet.
3. How many hands have you? 4. I have two hands. 5. How
many teachers have you (*pl.*)? 6. We have three teachers.
7. How many classes have you (*pl.*)? 8. We have four classes.
9. How many papers have I? 10. You have five papers. 11. In
the picture there are six Spanish women. 12. There are few
Frenchmen in the city.

C. *Divide, and underscore the accented syllable.* 1. clase
2. cuadro 3. maestro 4. papel 5. puerta 6. ventana 7. español
8. mucho

D. *Translate.* 1. Don't you speak Spanish, John? 2. No, sir,
I speak English. 3. Anna speaks Spanish a little. 4. Do you
(*pl.*) drink much water? 5. Yes, sir, we drink a great deal of
(much) water. 6. We eat a great deal of bread too. 7. Anna is
not at home today. 8. The other girls are at home. 9. One of the
boys is in front of the house. 10. The other is behind the house.
11. Mr. López's house has seven doors and many windows.
12. Mr. López has eight children (**hijos**). 13. Three of the children are out of the city. 14. Miss Anna López still lives in
Madrid. 15. How many books are there on the table? 16. There
are nine on the table and ten against the wall. 17. Are you going
home, John? 18. Not yet, Miss López.

Vocabulary

NOUNS

la clase, the class; the classroom; the kind
el cuadro, the picture
el maestro, the teacher
la muchacha, the girl
el papel, the paper
la pluma, the pen
la puerta, the door
la ventana, the window

ADJECTIVES

¿cuánto -a? how much? *pl.,* how many?
español -a, Spanish; *noun,* Spanish, Spaniard
francés -a, French; *noun,* French, Frenchman

inglés -a, English; *noun,* English, Englishman
mucho -a, much; *pl.,* many
otro -a, other, another
poco -a, little; *pl.,* few; *adv.,* little

VERB

hablar, to speak, talk

ADVERB

todavía, yet, still

PREPOSITIONS

contra, against
delante de, in front of
detrás de, behind
sobre, on, upon

OPTIONAL VOCABULARY

alemán -a, German	portugués -a, Portuguese
italiano -a, Italian	la tinta, the ink
el lápiz (*pl.*, lápices), the pencil	

Refrán

Quien mucho habla, mucho yerra.
He who talks much errs much.

Lección Quinta

(FIFTH LESSON)

IDIOMS

a casa de (mi tío), to (my uncle's)
¿cuántos años tiene (su tío)? how old is (your uncle)?
en casa de (mi tío), at (my uncle's)
junto a, by, beside
tener (cinco) años, to be (five) years old
tiene los ojos llenos de lágrimas, her (his, your) eyes are full of tears

---

Hoy toda la familia está en casa. Los padres están sentados a la mesa. Juan y su hermana están sentados [1] junto a la ventana. Hablan de sus tíos. Sus tíos viven en el campo, no muy lejos de la ciudad. Juan y su hermana están tristes, porque su tía está muy mala. Sus padres también están tristes. Su madre tiene los ojos llenos de lágrimas.

— ¿Por qué están Vds. tristes, Juan?
— Estamos tristes porque nuestra tía está mala.
— ¿Adónde van Vds.?
— Vamos a casa de nuestros tíos.
— ¿Van Vds. a pie?
— Sí, señor, vamos a pie.

---

[1] When an adjective modifies two nouns of different genders, use the masculine plural.

— ¿Cuántos años tiene Vd., Juan?
— Tengo dieciséis.
— ¿Cuántos años tiene su hermana?
— Mi hermana tiene once.
— Y su hermano, ¿cuántos años tiene?
— No tengo hermano, señor.

24. The Possessive Adjectives

SINGULAR	PLURAL		SINGULAR	PLURAL	
mi	mis, *my*		nuestro -a	nuestros -as, *our*	
tu	tus, *your* (fam.)		vuestro -a	vuestros -as, *your* (fam.)	
su	sus, *your, his, her, its*		su	sus,	*your, their*

The possessive adjective in Spanish agrees with the thing possessed. It is generally repeated before each noun modified.

mi padre y mi madre,   *my father and mother*
sus libros y sus papeles,   *your books and papers*
nuestros hijos y nuestras hijas,   *our sons and daughters*

25. Redundant Construction

Since **su** (**sus**) has several possible meanings, an explanatory prepositional phrase is often added in order to avoid ambiguity. **su libro de ella,** *her book.* However, in such cases it is better to use the definite article in place of **su** and add the prepositional phrase.

$$
\text{Tengo el libro} \begin{cases} \text{de Vd.} \\ \text{de él} \\ \text{de ella} \\ \text{de ellos} \end{cases} I\ have \begin{cases} your \\ his \\ her \\ their \end{cases} book
$$

26. Special Use of the Plural

The plural of a masculine noun often stands for a masculine singular and a feminine singular.

mis tíos,   *my uncle and aunt*
sus padres,   *his parents*
los reyes,   *the king and queen*

27. Cardinal Numbers (*continued*)

11 once	22 veintidós (veinte y dos)
12 doce	23 veintitrés (veinte y tres)
13 trece	24 veinticuatro (veinte y cuatro)
14 catorce	25 veinticinco (veinte y cinco)
15 quince	26 veintiséis (veinte y seis)
16 dieciséis (diez y seis)	27 veintisiete (veinte y siete)
17 diecisiete (diez y siete)	28 veintiocho (veinte y ocho)
18 dieciocho (diez y ocho)	29 veintinueve (veinte y nueve)
19 diecinueve (diez y nueve)	30 treinta
20 veinte	31 treinta y uno[1]
21 veintiuno (veinte y uno)	32 treinta y dos

Exercises

A. *Answer in Spanish.* 1. ¿Dónde está toda la familia hoy? 2. ¿Quiénes están sentados a la mesa? 3. ¿Dónde están sentados los hijos? 4. ¿De quiénes hablan? 5. ¿Dónde viven los tíos? 6. ¿Por qué está triste la familia? 7. ¿Quién tiene los ojos llenos de lágrimas? 8. ¿Adónde van Juan y su hermana? 9. ¿Van a caballo? 10. ¿Cuántos años tiene Juan? 11. ¿Cuántos años tiene su hermana? 12. ¿Cuántos años tiene Vd.?

B. *Read aloud in Spanish.* 1. my class 2. my teachers 3. your picture 4. your papers 5. his pen 6. his books 7. our house 8. our hands 9. their feet 10. our town

C. *Copy, supplying the correct answers.* 1. uno y ocho = 2. nueve y dos = 3. siete y cinco = 4. diez y tres = 5. ocho y seis = 6. siete y ocho = 7. doce y cuatro = 8. once y seis = 9. trece y cinco = 10. catorce y seis = 11. quince y siete = 12. veintiuno y cinco = 13. veintitrés y seis = 14. veinticuatro y siete =

D. *Translate.* 1. Where is your mother today, John? 2. She is in the country, at my uncle's. 3. My uncle is very sick. 4. Your sister's eyes are full of tears. 5. She is very sad, because

[1] The one-word forms are not used above 20 (veintinueve).

our mother is not at home. 6. Is your father out of the city too?
7. My father and mother are out of town (out of the city).
8. They are together in the country. 9. How old is your uncle?
10. My uncle is thirty-one and my aunt is twenty-nine. 11. My
uncle's house is full today. 12. The whole family is at home.
13. Who is seated by the window? 14. Mr. Pérez and his son are
seated by the window. 15. His two sisters are seated near the
door.

Vocabulary

NOUNS

el año, the year
el campo, the country, field
la familia, the family
lá hermana, the sister
el hermano, the brother
la lágrima, the tear
la madre, the mother
el ojo, the eye
el padre, the father
la tía, the aunt
el tío, the uncle

RELATIVE PRONOUN[1]

que, who, which, that

ADJECTIVES

junto -a, together (see *Idioms*)
lleno -a, full
malo -a, bad; *with* estar, ill, sick

sentado -a, seated
todo -a, all, whole, every
triste, sad

CONJUNCTION

porque, because

INTERROGATIVES

¿por qué? why?
¿quién? (*pl.*, **¿quiénes?**), who?
whom?

OPTIONAL VOCABULARY

la abuela, the grandmother
el abuelo, the grandfather
ia prima, the cousin (*f.*)
el primo, the cousin (*m.*)
la silla, the chair

Refrán

Más ven cuatro ojos que dos.
Two heads are better than one (Four eyes see more than two).

---

[1] See § 136.

Repaso

A. *Divide into syllables and write accent, if required. The stressed vowel is underscored.* 1. bonito 2. joven 3. importar 4. querer 5. lagrima 6. ellos 7. bueno 8. alli 9. estudios 10. dias 11. costumbre 12. nuestro 13. rapido 14. relacion 15. despues 16. compañia 17. correr 18. ejemplo

B. *Read aloud in Spanish, then write.* 1. one, three, five, seven, nine, eleven, thirteen, fifteen, seventeen, nineteen, twenty-one, twenty-three, twenty-five, twenty-seven, twenty-nine 2. two, four, six, eight, ten, twelve, fourteen, sixteen, eighteen, twenty, twenty-two, twenty-four, twenty-six, twenty-eight, thirty, thirty-two

C. *Translate.* 1. the horse's foot 2. Mr. Castro's house 3. Mrs. Castro's family 4. General Grant's history 5. twenty years of peace 6. other boys 7. How much water? 8. How many eyes? 9. How much bread? 10. How many parts? 11. few actions 12. many kings

D. *Translate.* 1. Anna is nine years old. 2. How old is her brother? 3. He is sixteen. 4. Are they still living in the country? 5. No, Miss Ortiz, they live in the village. 6. Why are you sad, John? 7. Your eyes are full of tears. 8. My parents are sick. 9. Is your sister at home? 10. She is at Mary's today. 11. Mary's house is outside of the city. 12. It is not far from the fountain. 13. What have you in your hand? 14. I have paper and two pens. 15. The books are on the table, near the door. 16. Anna is seated at the table. 17. The other girls are seated by the window. 18. Against the wall, there is a picture. 19. There is another picture behind the door. 20. Of what are the gentlemen talking? 21. They are talking of the war. 22. Where is there peace and justice? 23. There is peace and justice in our country. 24. John, aren't you taking meat today? 25. Yes, and I'm taking coffee too. 26. Does your mother drink wine? 27. Very little. She drinks a great deal of (much) water. 28. Are you (*pl.*) going to class? 29. There is no class today. 30. Why? Because the teacher's sons are going to Spain. 31. They speak Spanish and French. 32. They never speak English at home.

Lección Sexta

(SIXTH LESSON)

IDIOMS

tener que (escribir), to have to (write)
ya no, no longer

— ¿Quién tiene mi pluma?

— Yo la tengo aquí, Juan. ¿La quiere Vd.?

— Sí, la quiero. Tengo que escribir una carta. ¿Tiene Vd. ahí el papel también?

— No, señor, no lo tengo. El papel está allí sobre la mesa. ¿A quién escribe Vd.?

— Escribo a Carlos Morales y a su hermana.

— ¿Son españoles?

— Sí, son españoles. Son de Madrid. Él es muy bueno y muy rico. Ella es muy buena y muy bonita. Son buenos amigos de la familia. Su padre es autor, pero ya no escribe porque es muy viejo.

— ¿Es rico el padre del señor Morales?

— No, señor, no es rico. No es pobre tampoco.

— ¿Es Vd. rico, Juan?

— ¿Yo? No, señor, yo soy pobre. Bien lo sabe Vd.

— Sí, lo sé. Vd. y yo somos pobres, pero no importa, porque somos jóvenes.

27

28. The Subject Pronouns

yo,	*I*	nosotros -as,	*we*
tú,	*you* (fam.)	vosotros -as,	*you* (fam.)
usted,	*you*	ustedes,	*you*
él,	*he*	ellos,	*they* (m.)
ella,	*she*	ellas,	*they* (f.)

29. Uses of the Subject Pronouns

As previously noted (§ 15), the personal subject pronouns (except **usted**) are usually omitted in Spanish. They are used (a) for emphasis or (b) to make the meaning clear.

(a) ¿Quién tiene la pluma?   *Who has the pen?*
     Yo la tengo.   *I have it.*
(b) Él es rico y ella es bonita.   *He is rich and she is pretty.*
     ¿Quién llama a la puerta?   *Who is knocking at the door?*
     Es ella.   *It is she.*
     Soy yo.   *It is I.*

30. Direct Object Pronouns Referring to Things

MASCULINE	lo, *it*	los, *them*
FEMININE	la, *it*	las, *them*

When **lo**, *it*, refers to more than one word (to an idea), it is neuter. These pronouns stand immediately before the verb.[1]

Tengo el libro. Lo tengo.	*I have the book. I have it.*
Escribe la carta. La escribe.	*He writes the letter. He writes it.*
Quiero los cuadros. Los quiero.	*I want the pictures. I want them.*
Quiere las plumas. Las quiere.	*He wants the pens. He wants them.*
Es pobre. Sí, lo sé.	*He is poor. Yes, I know it.*

31. Present Indicative of *ser*, *to be*

(yo) soy,	*I am*	(nosotros) somos,	*we are*
(tú) eres,	*you are*	(vosotros) sois,	*you are*
(él) es,	*he is*	(ellos) son,	*they are*

---

[1] Except in a few cases to be learned later.

32. Uses of *ser* and *estar*

Spanish has two verbs meaning *to be*. **ser** is always used to connect two nouns or a pronoun and a noun.

> Su padre es autor.[1]   *His father is an author.*
> Ellos son españoles.   *They are Spaniards.*

estar is used to indicate *location* (*to be* in a place).

> El vino está en la mesa.   *The wine is on the table.*

(a) When a predicate adjective expresses a *state* or *condition*, **estar** must be used. (b) When a predicate adjective expresses an essential or characteristic *quality* of the subject, **ser** must be used. (c) Since certain adjectives may express either a condition or a quality, they have one meaning with **estar** and another with **ser**.

(a) **La casa está llena.**   *The house is full.*
    Ana está triste.   *Anna is sad.*
(b) **Ana es bonita.**   *Anna is pretty.*
    Los autores son ricos.[2]   *The authors are rich.*
    La casa es vieja.   *The house is old.*
(c) **Carlos está malo.**   *Charles is sick* (condition).
    Carlos es malo.   *Charles is bad* (characteristic quality).
    María está buena.   *Mary is well.*
    María es buena.   *Mary is good.*

33. The Adverbs *aquí, ahí,* and *allí*

aquí, *here,* presents no difficulty, but care must be exercised to distinguish between **ahí,** *there* (near the person spoken to), and **allí,** *there, over there* (at some distance). Adverbs should be placed as close as possible to the verb modified. When stressed, they usually follow the verb.

---

[1] The indefinite article is omitted in Spanish before a predicate noun that merely indicates the class (race, profession, occupation) to which the subject belongs.

[2] As predicate adjectives referring to persons, **rico, pobre, joven,** and **viejo** are used with the force of nouns, and, therefore, take the verb **ser**. **Son ricos.** *They are rich* (*men*). **Es viejo.** *He is old* (*an old man*).

ser = to express from which — (origin)

Aquí no hay pluma.	*There is no pen here.*
Yo la tengo aquí.	*I have it here.*
¿Tiene Vd. ahí el papel?	*Have you the paper there?*
Está allí sobre la mesa.	*It is over there on the table.*

34. Present Indicative of *saber* and *querer*

saber		querer	
to know; to know how (can)		*to wish, want; to will*	
sé	sabemos	quiero	queremos
sabes	sabéis	quieres	queréis
sabe	saben	quiere	quieren

Exercises

A. *Answer in Spanish.* 1. ¿Sabe Vd. quién tiéne la pluma de Juan? 2. ¿Quién la quiere? 3. ¿Por qué la quiere? 4. ¿A quién quiere escribir la carta? 5. ¿De qué ciudad son Carlos y su hermana? 6. ¿Quién es autor? 7. ¿Por qué no escribe? 8. ¿Quién es rico? 9. ¿Quién es pobre? 10. ¿Por qué no importa?

B. *Translate (pronouns refer to nouns in parentheses).* 1. (**café**) I take it. 2. (**agua**) Are you drinking it? 3. (**pan**) He is eating it. 4. (**carne**) We eat it. 5. (**vino**) You (*pl.*) drink it. 6. (**libros**) They have them. 7. (**plumas**) He wants them. 8. (**cuadros**) We want them. 9. (**español**) Do you speak it? 10. (**cartas**) We write them.

C. *Translate.* 1. The young man who lives here is an author. 2. He writes many books, and he writes well. 3. Do he and his sister know that their father is ill? 4. He knows it, but she doesn't know it. 5. What have you there in your hand? 6. It is a letter from Madrid, from my friend Charles. 7. Are your parents going to Madrid? 8. My parents are already there. 9. I wish to go to Spain too, but I am poor. 10. You are not rich either. 11. Yes, I know it, but it doesn't matter. 12. I have to go to my uncle's today. 13. Does your uncle still have twelve horses? 14. No, my uncle no longer has horses. 15. Can you (Do you know how to) write in Spanish? 16. Yes, and I can write in French, too.

Vocabulary

NOUNS

el amigo (la amiga), the friend
Carlos, Charles
la carta, the letter

ADJECTIVES

bonito -a, pretty
bueno -a, good; *with* estar, well
joven, young; *noun*, young man,
    young woman
pobre, poor; *noun*, poor man
rico -a, rich; *noun*, rich man
viejo -a, old; *noun*, old man, old
    woman

VERBS

escribir, to write
importar, to matter; to be impor-
    tant
querer, to wish, want; to will
saber, to know; to know how

ADVERBS

ahí, there (*near by*)
allí, there, over there
aquí, here
bien, well
ya, now, already

CONJUNCTIONS

pero, but
que, that
tampoco, neither, either

OPTIONAL VOCABULARY

feo -a, ugly, homely
enfermo -a, ill, sick
interesante, interesting

Refrán

La verdad, aunque severa, es amiga verdadera.
Truth, though severe, is a faithful friend.

Lección Séptima

(SEVENTH LESSON)

IDIOMS

es verdad, it is true
¿no es verdad? *or* ¿verdad? isn't it so? doesn't he? *etc.*
pues entonces, well then
Sí, lo sé, Yes, I know
todos los días, every day

— ¿Qué es eso, Pepe?

— Es una carta para Juan. Son para él también estos libros. Los llevo a su casa. ¿Quiere Vd. venir conmigo, Luis?

— Ahora no, Pepe. Busco a Carlos. Me ayuda con mis estudios. También le ayuda a Vd., ¿no es verdad?

— Sí, me ayuda a mí y a mi hermano. Nos ayuda casi todos los días. ¿Sabe Vd. que mi hermano ya habla español muy bien?

— Sí, ya lo sé. Su hermano estudia mucho, ¿verdad?

— Sí, estudia mucho; lee mucho y habla mucho. Sabe muchas ⁞ ꭤras.

Pues adiós, Pepe. Allí veo a Carlos.

— ¿Dónde? Yo no le veo.

— Está con su padre. Ahora no los vemos, porque están detrás de aquellos árboles.

— Pues entonces, adiós, Luis.

35. Demonstrative Adjectives

SINGULAR			PLURAL		
este,	esta,	*this*	estos,	estas,	*these*
ese,	esa,	*that* (near by)	esos,	esas,	*those* (near by)
aquel,	aquella,	*that* (yonder)	aquellos,	aquellas,	*those* (yonder)

These demonstrative adjectives correspond to the adverbs **aquí, ahí, allí.**

este libro (aquí)	*this book* (*here*)
esa pluma (ahí)	*that pen* (*there*, near the person addressed)
aquella carta (allí)	*that letter* (*over there, yonder*)
aquel día	*that day* (some time ago)

36. Demonstrative Pronouns

The above forms have a written accent when used as pronouns.
éste, *this* (*one*) **ése**, *that* (*one*) **aquél**, *that* (*one,* yonder)

Hay dos cartas. Ésta es para	*There are two letters. This one is for*
Vd.; aquélla es para Juan.	*you; that one is for John.*

The neuter forms **esto, eso,** and **aquello** refer to a preceding statement, a general idea, or an object not yet identified. They do not require an accent, since there are no neuter adjectives.

Esto es verdad.	*This* (that I am saying) *is true.*
Eso es.	*That's it* (the idea).
¿Qué es eso?	*What is that* (thing not yet identified)?

37. Direct Object Pronouns Referring to Persons [1]

SINGULAR		PLURAL	
me,	*me*	nos,	*us*
te,	*you* (fam.)	os,	*you* (fam.)
le,	*him; you* (m.)	los,	*them;* los or ~~les~~ *you* (m.)
la,	*her; you* (f.)	las,	*them; you* (f.)

---

[1] For table of personal pronouns see § 133.

Remember that object pronouns are placed immediately before the verb.

Me ayuda.	*He helps me.*
Nos ven.	*They see us.*
No los veo.	*I do not see them.*

38. Prepositional Forms of the Object Pronouns

The forms used after a preposition are the same as the subject pronouns, except in the first and second persons singular (**mí, ti**). With the preposition **con, mí** and **ti** become **conmigo,** *with me,* and **contigo,** *with you* (fam.)

SINGULAR		PLURAL	
para mí,	*for me*	**para nosotros -as,** *for us*	
para ti,	*for you* (fam.)	**para vosotros -as,** *for you* (fam.)	
para usted, *for you*		**para ustedes,**	*for you*
para él,	*for him, it*	**para ellos,**	*for them* (m.)
para ella,	*for her, it*	**para ellas,**	*for them* (f.)

39. Redundant Construction

The prepositional forms of the object pronouns are stressed forms. They are often used, with the preposition **a,** to make clear the meaning of the unstressed forms (§37). They are also used for emphasis or contrast.

Le ayudo $\begin{cases} \textbf{a Vd.} \\ \textbf{a él} \end{cases}$ *I help* $\begin{cases} you \\ him \end{cases}$

Carlos le ayuda a Vd., ¿verdad?	*Charles helps you, doesn't he?*
Me ayuda a mí y a mi hermano.	*He helps me and my brother.*
Le busco a él, a ella no.	*I am looking for him, not her.*

40. The "Personal" *a*

A peculiar characteristic of Spanish is the use of **a** before a noun object when the object is a definite person or a personified thing. Note also **¿a quién?** *whom?*

¿A quién ve Vd.?   *Whom do you see?*
Veo a Juan.   *I see John.*
Juan ayuda al señor Pérez. *John is helping Mr. Pérez.*

41. Present Indicative of *ver* and *venir*

ver		venir	
to see		*to come*	
veo	vemos	vengo	venimos
ves	veis	vienes	venís
ve	ven	viene	vienen

Exercises

A. *Answer in Spanish.* 1. ¿Para quién es la carta que tiene Pepe? 2. ¿Adónde lleva Pepe los libros? 3. ¿Por qué no va con él Luis? 4. ¿Quién le ayuda con sus estudios? 5. ¿Quién estudia mucho? 6. ¿Quién lee muchos libros en español? 7. ¿Estudia Vd. mucho? 8. ¿Lee Vd. libros en español? 9. ¿Sabe Vd. muchas palabras? 10. ¿A quién ve Luis? 11. ¿Con quién está Carlos? 12. ¿Por qué no los ve Pepe?

B. *Translate.* 1. Do you help this boy? Yes, I help him. 2. Do you want these papers? No, I don't want them. 3. Are you taking that meat home? Yes, I am taking it home. 4. I want those books that you have in your hand. I want them. 5. I do not see my father. He is behind those trees. 6. Will you take (¿**Quiere Vd. llevar**) this bread to that girl? 7. Will you come with me now? 8. Not now. I am going with them. 9. Have you letters for us? 10. These letters are for her.

C. *Translate.* 1. I wish to read this letter and that one. 2. What's this, don't you wish to go with me? 3. Not now. I have to look for my friend Charles. 4. There he is, beside that tree. 5. Well then, good-by, Joe. 6. Louis knows many words in Spanish, doesn't he? 7. He speaks Spanish with Mr. Morales every day. 8. Will you (*pl.*) come with me to my uncle's? 9. We have to take these pictures home. 10. Will you take those home too? 11. My father doesn't want those pictures. 12. That is not true, well you know it. 13. I come here every day. 14. You come on foot, don't you? 15. No, sir, I come on horseback. 16. My horse is sick. Yes, I know it.

Vocabulary

NOUNS

el árbol, the tree
el día, the day
el estudio, the study
Luis, Louis
la palabra, the word
Pepe, Joe
la verdad, the truth

VERBS

ayudar, to help
buscar, to look for
estudiar, to study
leer, to read
llevar, to take,[1] carry
venir, to come
ver, to see

ADVERBS

ahora, now
casi, almost, nearly
entonces, then

PREPOSITIONS

con, with
para, for; in order to; to

INTERJECTIONS

adiós, good-by
pues, well (then)

OPTIONAL VOCABULARY

la hoja, the leaf; sheet (of paper)
verde, green

Refrán

Aquellos son ricos que tienen amigos.
They (those) are rich who have friends.

---

[1] Be careful to distinguish between llevar, *to take* (*carry, transport*), and tomar, *to take, eat, drink*.

Lección Octava

(EIGHTH LESSON)

IDIOMS

acaba de (entrar), he has just (entered)
de modo que, so, so that
de (este) modo, in (this) way
entrar en relaciones con, to enter into
    (establish) business connections with
la señora de[1] **(Morales),** Mrs. (Morales)
por eso, therefore; for that reason
todo el día, all day

ANA: ¿De modo que Vds. aprenden a hablar español?

LUIS: Sí, Ana, yo y toda la familia. La señora de Morales nos enseña a leer, escribir y hablar. Al terminar nuestros estudios vamos a Méjico.[2] Mi padre acaba de entrar en relaciones con una casa de ese país. Vamos a pasar un año con nuestros vecinos al otro lado del Río Grande.

ANA: ¡Ya comprendo por qué Vd. trabaja todo el día!

LUIS: Pues, para comprender la vida y las costumbres de nuestros vecinos hay que vivir entre ellos y hablarles en español, ¿no es verdad?

---

[1] The preposition **de** is often omitted.
[2] In Mexico, for historical reasons, spelled with an **x** (**México**), but pronounced **Méjico.**

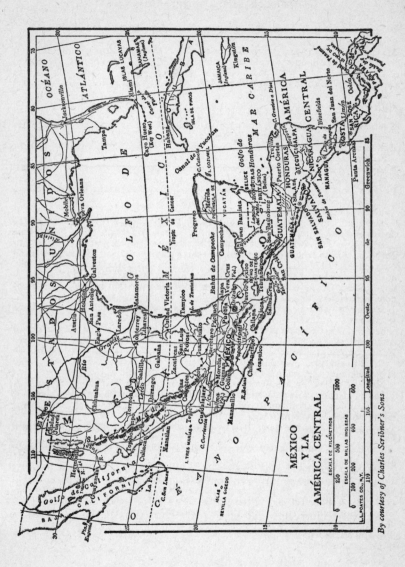

MÉXICO Y LA
AMÉRICA CENTRAL

By courtesy of Charles Scribner's Sons

Mexico and Central America

(Méjico y la América Central)

Mexico (pop. 16,522,722):[1] capital, Mexico, D. F. (*Distrito Federal*). Chief exports: petroleum and products, gold, silver, henequen, coffee, lead, copper, zinc, fruits, vegetables.

Costa Rica (pop. 591,862): capital, San José. Chief exports: coffee, bananas, cacao, hides, lumber.

El Salvador (pop. 1,459,578): capital, San Salvador. Chief exports: coffee, sugar, balsam, indigo.

Guatemala (pop. 2,466,227): capital, Guatemala. Chief exports: coffee, bananas, sugar, lumber, chicle, hides.

Honduras (pop. 962,685): capital, Tegucigalpa. Chief exports: bananas, leaf tobacco, mahogany, coffee, coconuts, cattle.

Nicaragua (pop. 1,133,572): capital, Managua. Chief exports: coffee, bananas, lumber, sugar.

Panama (pop. 467,459): capital, Panama. Chief exports: bananas, coconuts, cacao, mother-of-pearl shells.

The great central plateau of Mexico, 3,000 to 8,000 feet elevation, is called the **tierras templadas** (temperate lands). Areas above 8,000 feet are called **tierras frías** (cold lands). The lowlands that form a fringe between the coast and the mountains are called **tierras calientes** (hot lands). Because of these vertical climatic zones and her geographical position, Mexico probably has a greater diversity of plant life than any other country in the world. The central plateau has a number of lakes but no large rivers. Of the short rivers that flow from the mountain ranges into the sea, none is navigable throughout the year.

Mexico has about 44,000,000 acres of forests, mainly tropical, with such hardwoods as mahogany, ebony, and rosewood.

Because of her enormous mineral wealth, Mexico is potentially one of the richest countries in the world. Mining is the chief industry. She produces 40 per cent of the world's output of silver.

Cerro del Mercado, a mountain near the city of Durango in Mexico, is composed almost entirely of pure iron ore.

Mexico's chief ports are Veracruz and Tampico, both on the Gulf of Mexico.

Lake Petén in Guatemala contains thirty species of fish not found elsewhere.

El Salvador, smallest country of Central America (about the size of New Jersey), is the most densely populated of the American republics.

Little Costa Rica has more than twice as many species of birds as the whole of Europe.

Panama has neither army nor navy. Its independence is guaranteed by the United States.

Panama, capital and chief Pacific port of the republic of Panama, founded in 1519 by Pedro Arias de Ávila, is the oldest town founded by Europeans on the mainland of America. In the sixteenth century it was, with the exception of Cartagena, the strongest Spanish fortress in the New World. Gold and silver from Peru were carried from Panama across the Isthmus to Chagres for shipment to Spain.

Columbus first landed on the American continent in 1502 at Cape Honduras. The first settlement in Honduras was made by Christóbal de Olid in 1524, by order of Hernando Cortés.

-----

[1] All population figures are from *The World Almanac* for 1939.

ANA: ¡Naturalmente! Sin hablar la lengua del país no **vamos** a comprender a nuestros vecinos.

LUIS: Por eso, trabajo mucho; por eso le hablo a Vd. en **es-**pañol. Quiero hablar bien antes de salir para Méjico.

ANA: ¿Habla bien su hermano?

LUIS: Habla mal, pero lee y escribe bien.

42. Uses of the Infinitive.

1. The infinitive is used after a preposition.

> **antes de salir** *before leaving*
> **sin hablar** *without speaking*

2. When *to* of the English infinitive means *in order to*, **para** must be used in Spanish.

Para aprender hay que trabajar mucho. *To learn one must work hard.*

After a verb of motion, **a** may be substituted for **para**.

Viene a hablar con mi padre. *He comes to talk with my father.*

3. **al** with an infinitive equals English *on* with a present participle.

> **al terminar mis estudios** *on finishing my studies*
> **al salir** *on leaving*

4. The infinitive follows many Spanish verbs without an intervening preposition, just as in English.

> **Quiere hablar.** *He wishes to speak.*
> **Sé leer.** *I know how to read.*

But a number of verbs require a preposition. The preposition should be learned with the verb. Verbs of motion and verbs meaning *to begin*, *to teach*, and *to learn* take **a** before a following infinitive.

> **Voy a escribir una carta.** *I am going to write a letter.*
> **Me enseña a leer.** *He teaches me to read.*
> **Aprendo a hablar.** *I am learning to speak.*

comenzar
empezar *a*
principiar

comienzo a estudiar

43. The Expression *hay que*

When the construction is impersonal, **hay que** (not **tener que**) is used to express necessity.

> **Hay que trabajar.** *One must work.*
> **Hay que ayudarle.** *It is necessary to help him.*

44. Indirect Object Pronouns

SINGULAR	PLURAL
me, *to me*	**nos**, *to us*
te, *to you* (fam.)	**os**, *to you* (fam.)
le, *to you, him, her*	**les**, *to you, them*

We have learned (§§ 30 and 37) that object pronouns stand immediately before the verb. However, when an object pronoun (direct or indirect) is the object of an infinitive, it follows the infinitive as an added syllable.

Nos enseña el cuadro.	*He shows us the picture.*
Quiero hablarle a ella.	*I want to speak to her.*
Voy a escribirles una carta.	*I am going to write a letter to them.*
No les importa a Vds., ¿verdad?	*It doesn't matter to you, does it?*

45. Adverbs in *-mente*

Many adverbs are formed by adding **-mente** (English *-ly*) to the feminine singular of the adjective.[1]

bonito -a,	*pretty*	**bonitamente,**	*prettily*
triste,	*sad*	**tristemente,**	*sadly*
natural,	*natural*	**naturalmente,**	*naturally*

The addition of **-mente** does not affect the accent.

rápido -a,	*rapid, quick*	**rápidamente,**	*rapidly, quickly*
fácil,	*easy*	**fácilmente,**	*easily*

---

[1] When two or more adverbs of this type modify the same word, each form is feminine but -mente is used with the last one only: **Escribe rápida y fácilmente.** *He writes rapidly and easily.*

46. Present Indicative of *salir*, *to leave, go out*

salgo	salimos
sales	salís
sale	salen

Exercises

A. *Answer in Spanish.* 1. ¿Quién aprende a hablar español? 2. ¿Quién le enseña a hablar? 3. Al terminar sus estudios, ¿adónde van Luis y su familia? 4. ¿Con qué casa acaba de entrar en relaciones el padre? 5. ¿Cuántos años van a pasar en Méjico? 6. ¿De qué vecinos habla Luis? 7. ¿Qué río está entre nosotros y estos vecinos? 8. Para comprender la vida y las costumbres de los mejicanos, ¿dónde hay que vivir? 9. ¿Qué lengua hay que hablar? 10. ¿Aprende Vd. fácilmente? 11. ¿Quién trabaja todo el día para aprender español? 12. Antes de salir para Méjico, ¿qué quiere saber bien Luis? 13. ¿Habla bien el hermano de Luis? 14. ¿Lee y escribe mal también?

B. *Translate (use the redundant construction when necessary for emphasis or clearness).* 1. She writes to me and I write to her. 2. He wishes to speak to us. 3. Will you (**¿Quiere Vd.**) show me the letter? 4. I have just read the letter to you. 5. Will you take these papers to them? 6. On establishing (business) connections with that house. 7. Before leaving (**salir de**) the house. 8. Without speaking to you (*pl.*) of these customs.

C. *Translate.* 1. So Mrs. Morales is teaching you to speak Spanish? 2. That's it. I am also learning to read. 3. I wish to understand the life and customs of my neighbors. 4. My uncle is going to establish connections with a house in (**de**) Mexico. 5. Is it for that reason that he is going to spend a year on the other side of the Rio Grande? 6. Yes, that's it. One must study in Mexico to understand the Mexicans. 7. Before leaving for Mexico he is coming to see you (*pl.*). 8. Of course! We are very good friends. 9. On entering the house we see Charles. 10. We do not speak to him because he has to work. 11. Charles learns rapidly. 12. Where are the other boys? 13. There they are, near the river. 14. One of them is going to spend a year in Madrid. 15. Is he going to Spain without knowing how to speak Spanish? 16. Among his friends there are two Spaniards. 17. They are teaching him to speak and to write. 18. One of those boys has just finished a book. 19. Will you show me that book? 20. I have it at home and you are going with me, aren't you?

Vocabulary

NOUNS

la costumbre, custom, habit [1]
la lengua, tongue, language
el modo, way, manner
la relación, relation; *pl.*, (business) relations, connections
el río, river
el vecino, neighbor
la vida, life

comprender, to understand
enseñar (a), to show; to teach
entrar (en), to enter, go in, come in
pasar, to pass; to happen; to spend (*time*)
salir (de), to leave, go out
terminar, to finish, end
trabajar, to work

ADJECTIVES

fácil, easy
rápido -a, rapid, quick

ADVERBS

mal, badly
naturalmente, naturally, of course

VERBS

acabar, to finish; *with* de *and an inf.*, to have just . . .
aprender (a), [2] to learn

PREPOSITIONS

antes de, before (*time*)
entre, between, among

[1] From this point on, the definite article will not be translated in the vocabularies. It will be used merely to indicate gender.
[2] The preposition required before a following infinitive or before a noun object will be shown in parentheses.

PREPOSITIONS	OPTIONAL VOCABULARY
por, for, by, through, along	**difícil,** difficult
sin, without	**lento -a,** slow

Refrán

Come pan y bebe agua, y vivirás vida larga.
Eat bread and drink water, and you will live a long life.

Lección Novena

(NINTH LESSON)

IDIOMS

al fin, finally, at last
echar a (la calle), to throw into (the street)

Pepe y Luis entran en el teatro. Hay mucha gente, pero al fin encuentran sitio cerca de la escena.

LUIS: ¿Oye Vd. bien, Pepe?

PEPE: Sí, oigo bien, pero no entiendo. Ese joven habla muy rápidamente.

LUIS: Pues yo le entiendo. El viejo a quien habla es su padre. El hijo le pide dinero.

PEPE: ¿No quiere dárselo?

LUIS: No se lo da, porque el hijo no quiere trabajar. Pasa todo el día en el café. Bebe mucho y pierde mucho dinero. El dueño del café acaba de echarle a la calle, porque ya no tiene dinero. Ahora quiere engañar a su padre. En una palabra, el hijo es un joven muy malo.

PEPE: ¿Cómo sabe Vd. todo eso?

LUIS: No puedo decírselo ahora. Es mala costumbre hablar en el teatro.

PEPE: No importa. Puede Vd. decírmelo al fin del acto.

45

47. Radical-Changing Verbs

In many Spanish verbs, the stem-vowel **o** becomes **ue** when stressed. Likewise **e** becomes **ie**. Note that the vowel does not change in the first and second persons plural, since the stem-vowel is not stressed. A few **-ir** verbs change **e** to **i** under stress. In the vocabulary, radical-changing verbs will be indicated thus: **(ue)**, **(ie)**, **(i)**. (See §§ 129, 130, 131.)

encontrar (ue)	entender (ie)	pedir (i)
to meet, find	*to understand*	*to ask for*
encuentro	entiendo	pido
encuentras	entiendes	pides
encuentra	entiende	pide
encontramos	entendemos	pedimos
encontráis	entendéis	pedís
encuentran	entienden	piden

48. Two Object Pronouns

When there are two object pronouns, the indirect precedes the direct. Note that the infinitive always has a written accent when two pronouns are added.

Tiene el dinero, pero no me lo da.	*He has the money, but he doesn't give it to me.*
No quiere dármelo.	*He won't give it to me.*
¿Va a escribirles una carta?	*Is he going to write you* (pl.) *a letter?*
Nos la escribe ahora.	*He is writing it to us now.*

When both object pronouns are third person, **se** is used instead of **le** or **les** as indirect object. Unless the meaning of **se** is made clear by the context, the redundant construction should be used.

Se lo digo a él (a ella, a Vd., etc.).	*I tell it to him* (*to her, to you,* etc.).
Se los pido a Vds.	*I ask you for them.*
¿Quiere Vd. dárselo (a ellos)?	*Will you give it to them?*

49. Present Indicative of *dar*, *decir*, and *oír*

dar *to give*	decir *to say, tell*	oír *to hear*
doy	digo	oigo
das	dices	oyes
da	dice	oye
damos	decimos	oímos
dais	decís	oís
dan	dicen	oyen

Exercises

A. *Answer in Spanish.* 1. Al entrar en el teatro, ¿qué buscan Pepe y Luis? 2. ¿Por qué toman sitio cerca de la escena? 3. ¿Por qué no entiende Pepe? 4. ¿A quién habla el joven en la escena? 5. ¿Qué le [1] pide a su padre el hijo? 6. ¿Por qué no se lo da el padre? 7. ¿Dónde pasa el joven todo el día? 8. ¿Qué pierde todos los días? 9. ¿Quién acaba de echarle a la calle? 10. ¿Por qué le echa a la calle? 11. ¿A quién quiere engañar el hijo? 12. En una palabra, ¿qué clase de hijo es? 13. ¿Qué quiere saber Pepe? 14. ¿Por qué no se lo dice Luis?

B. *Translate.* (*Object pronouns refer to nouns in parentheses.*) (**dinero**) 1. He gives it to me. 2. They give it to us. 3. I give it to you. 4. Will you give it to me? 5. I can't give it to you. — (**carta**) 6. I am writing it to her. 7. We are writing it to you (*pl.*). 8. He is writing it to them. 9. Will you read it to him? 10. I can't read it to him.

C. *Answer affirmatively, using two object pronouns.* (**libros**) 1. ¿Me los pide Vd.? 2. ¿Se los doy a Vd.? 3. ¿Nos los piden

---

[1] The use of a redundant pronoun is common, especially when the object is a person (see note 1, p. 64).

Vds.? 4. ¿Se los damos a Vds.? 5. ¿Va Vd. a llevárselos a ellos?
— (plumas) 6. ¿Se las da Vd. a él? 7. ¿Se las doy a ellas?
8. ¿Se las da a Vds. el maestro? 9. ¿Me las piden Vds.? 10. ¿Voy
a dárselas a Vds.?

D. *Translate.* 1. Our friends are looking for Joe. 2. He and
Louis have just entered the theater. 3. They are seated near the
stage. 4. There they can see and hear well. 5. The theater is
almost full. 6. There are still many people in the street who wish
to enter. 7. On the other side of the theater there are places for
three. 8. I hear well, but I don't understand all the words.
9. Well, one must know many words in order to understand.
10. What is happening (¿Qué pasa) on the stage? 11. The young
man meets his father in the street. 12. He asks for money.
13. His father does not give it to him. 14. The old man knows
that his son deceives him. 15. The son has bad habits. 16. He
loses much money every day. 17. Finally, the owner of the café
throws him into the street. 18. Can you tell me how the act
ends? 19. I am going to tell you [it] [1] now. 20. Louis has just
told me.

Vocabulary

NOUNS	VERBS
el **acto**, act	**dar**, to give
la **calle**, street	**decir**, to say, tell
el **dinero**, money	**echar**, to throw
el **dueño**, owner, proprietor	**encontrar** (ue), to meet; to find
la **escena**, scene, stage	**engañar**, to deceive
el **fin**, end	**entender** (ie), to understand
la **gente**, people	**oír**, to hear
el **sitio**, place	**pedir** (i), to ask for; to order
el **teatro**, theater	**perder** (ie), to lose; to waste
	poder (ue), to be able, can

---

[1] In English, *it* is frequently omitted. Do not omit in Spanish.

INTERROGATIVE

¿cómo? how?

OPTIONAL VOCABULARY

abajo, down, below; downstairs;
ir calle abajo, to go down the
street
arriba, above, up; upstairs; **ir
calle arriba,** to go up the street

Refrán

Quien mal dice, peor oye.
He who speaks evil, hears worse.

Lección Décima

IDIOMS

algunas veces, sometimes
gozar de, to enjoy
había, there was, there were
más allá, beyond, farther on
muchas veces, often

Ana vive ahora en una ciudad grande. Vive en una casa grande. Cuando era niña vivía en el campo, lejos de la ciudad. Sus padres tenían una casa pequeña cerca de un río. Desde la ventana de su cuarto Ana podía ver el río y, más allá, unas montañas altas y hermosas. Las montañas estaban cubiertas de árboles de todas clases.

Algunas veces Ana y su padre pasaban todo el día allá en las montañas. Gozaban del aire puro y bebían el agua fría de las fuentes. Entre los árboles había muchos animales pequeños. Ana y su padre los veían muchas veces, cuando venían a beber. Algunas veces, cuando los dos estaban sentados debajo de un árbol, veían tres o cuatro animales.

50. The Imperfect Indicative

The imperfect has only two sets of endings, one for **-ar** verbs

(aba, abas, aba, ábamos, abais, aban), and one for -er and -ir
verbs (ía, ías, ía, íamos, íais, ían).

hablar		comer		vivir	
hablaba	hablábamos	comía	comíamos	vivía	vivíamos
hablabas	hablabais	comías	comíais	vivías	vivíais
hablaba	hablaban	comía	comían	vivía	vivían

All verbs follow the above models with the exception of **ir, ser,**
and **ver.**

ir		ser		ver	
iba	íbamos	era	éramos	veía	veíamos
ibas	ibais	eras	erais	veías	veíais
iba	iban	era	eran	veía	veían

The imperfect may be translated in the following ways:

hablaba, *he was speaking, he used to speak, he spoke* (habitually)
era, *he was, he used to be*
iba, *he was going, he used to go, he went* (habitually)

51. Uses of the Imperfect

The imperfect tense is used to describe actions, states, or conditions in past time. It is often the equivalent of the English past
progressive (*was* or *were* with the present participle). However,
the imperfect is also required where English uses the simple past
tense, if habitual or recurrent action or a continuous state is indicated. Study the following examples carefully:

(a) Description:

La niña era bonita. *The child was pretty.*
La casa tenía tres puertas. *The house had three doors.*

(b) Action in progress:

El animal bebía el agua. *The animal was drinking the water.*

(c) State or condition prevailing:

El agua estaba fría.	*The water was cold.*
Luis estaba malo.	*Louis was sick.*

(d) Habitual or recurrent action (often expressed in English by
   used to or *would*):

Iban allá todos los días.	*They went (used to go) there every day.*
Algunas veces comían debajo de un árbol.	*Sometimes they would eat under a tree.*

(e) Time of day in the past:

Eran las cuatro de la tarde.	*It was four o'clock in the afternoon.*

52. Position of Adjectives

1. A descriptive adjective generally follows the noun it modifies. It always follows when it serves to distinguish a particular
person or thing from others of the same class.[1]

el aire puro de las montañas	*the pure air of the mountains*
una casa pequeña	*a small house* (not all houses are small)
los niños pobres	*the poor children* (as distinguished from rich children)
los pobres niños	*the poor* (unfortunate) *children*

2. Limiting adjectives (demonstrative adjectives, adjectives
expressing number, quantity, etc.) generally precede the noun.

aquellas montañas	*those mountains*
muchos animales	*many animals*
¿cuántos árboles?	*how many trees?*
dos fuentes	*two springs*

---

[1] A descriptive adjective precedes the noun when used figuratively, or when the
quality or condition it expresses is inherent. or considered as a fact of general
knowledge; **la blanca nieve,** *the white snow.*

Exercises

A. *Answer in Spanish.* 1. ¿Dónde vive Ana ahora? 2. ¿Dónde vivía cuando era niña? 3. ¿Era grande o pequeña la casa en que vivía? 4. ¿Qué podía ver desde la ventana de su cuarto? 5. ¿De qué estaban cubiertas las montañas? 6. ¿Dónde pasaban Ana y su padre todo el día muchas veces? 7. ¿De qué gozaban allá en las montañas? 8. ¿Dónde encontraban agua para beber? 9. ¿Qué había entre los árboles? 10. ¿Cuándo los veían Ana y su padre? 11. ¿Eran grandes o pequeños? 12. Cuando Ana estaba sentada debajo de un árbol, ¿qué veía algunas veces?

B. *Read aloud, then write, translating the italicized words.* 1. *I was eating* la carne. 2. *We were writing* una carta. 3. *He used to read* muchos libros. 4. *They were going* al río. 5. *You were losing* mucho dinero. 6. *Were you (pl.) deceiving* a los niños? 7. *I used to hear* las aguas de la fuente. 8. Lo *they were throwing* al agua. 9. ¿Qué *were you saying?* 10. *I used to meet* al viejo en la calle. 11. *There were* muchos animales. 12. El agua *was not* fría. 13. *There was no* sitio para los libros. 14. *It was* un teatro grande.

C. *Translate.* 1. When Louis was a child, he lived in a small town. 2. His uncle had a large house in the country. 3. He used to go to his uncle's nearly every day. 4. Behind the house there was a river. 5. Beyond, there was a tall mountain. 6. Louis and his aunt often spent the whole day in the mountains. 7. They enjoyed the pure air and drank the cold water of the springs. 8. They used to eat under a big tree. 9. They used to see the animals when they came to drink. 10. When they didn't come, Louis was sad. 11. There were no large animals there in the mountains. 12. Sometimes four or five little boys would go to the mountains with them. 13. Seated under a tree, they would eat the bread that Louis's mother gave them. 14. Louis's mother was very pretty. 15. Yes, I know it, and she was very good. 16. From here, I can see some beautiful fields. 17. Once (**una vez**), when I was a boy, those fields were covered with water. 18. The river passes through them.

Vocabulary

NOUNS

el aire, air
el animal, animal
el cuarto, room
María, Mary
la montaña, mountain
el niño, child, little boy; *f.*, child, little girl; *pl.*, children
la vez (*pl.*, veces [1]), time

ADJECTIVES

alguno -a, some; *pl.*, some, a few
alto -a, tall, high
cubierto -a, covered
frío -a, cold
grande, large, big
hermoso -a, beautiful
más, more; *adv.*, more (*see Idioms*)
pequeño -a, small, little
puro -a, pure
unos -as, some

VERB

gozar (de), to enjoy

ADVERBS

allá, there [2]
cuando, when

PREPOSITIONS

debajo de, under
desde, from, since

CONJUNCTION

o, or; o . . . o, either . . . or

OPTIONAL VOCABULARY

caliente, warm, hot
el chico, small boy, youngster
fresco -a, fresh, cool; agua fresca, cold water
la habitación, room, bedroom

Refrán

Contra amor y fortuna, no hay defensa alguna.
Against love and fortune there is no defense whatever.

---

[1] Nouns ending in z change z to c in the plural. See table in § 95 for spellings of the sound *th*.

[2] The place indicated by allá is less definite than that indicated by allí.

Repaso

A. *Copy, supplying the correct form of* **ser** *or* **estar** *and the adjective.* 1. El *poor* animal *is sick*. 2. *Some* costumbres *are good*, otras *are bad*. 3. *Those* niños *are* muy *pretty*. 4. La mesa *is covered* de dinero. 5. El dueño de *this* café *is sad*. 6. *That* escena *was beautiful*. 7. Vivíamos en *some* montañas muy *high*, porque *that* año mi madre no *was well*.

B. *Read aloud, translating the italicized words.* 1. Voy *with them*. 2. Ellos van *with me*. 3. La carta es *for her*. 4. Vive en esta calle, pero Vd. no puede pasar *through it*. 5. El cuarto era grande, pero no había mesa *in it*. 6. Mis hermanas no están aquí y no quiero entrar *without them*. 7. *Among us* no hay vecinos ricos. 8. ¿Estaban en la casa o *outside of it*?

C. *Object pronouns refer to nouns given in parentheses. Use the redundant construction for clearness or emphasis where necessary.* 1. (**carta**) He was writing it to her, not to me. 2. (**palabras**) I am going to read them to you. 3. (**acto**) He has just read it to me. 4. (**costumbres**) He is teaching them to us. 5. (**dinero**) Before giving it to him. 6. (**papeles**) On taking them to you (*pl.*). 7. (**plumas**) We were asking him for them. 8. (**libro**) Will you throw it to me?

D. *Use the subject pronouns only where necessary for clearness or emphasis.* 1. I don't understand you and he doesn't understand you either. 2. This young man understands because he is a teacher. 3. We are going to finish these letters before going home. 4. I do not hear the waters of the river. 5. From here, you can hear them easily. 6. I have to look for my father now. 7. There he is, under that tree. 8. He knows how to enjoy life. 9. That is true, but he wastes his money. 10. Who is the owner of those fields? 11. They belong to (**son de**) my uncle, who lives there in the mountains. 12. So you used to see him every day? 13. Of course. I used to enjoy the pure air of the mountains. 14. Sometimes I spent the whole day with him. 15. A neighbor's son used to work in my uncle's fields. 16. In these fields by the river? 17. In these or in those on the other side. 18. He is a small boy, but it doesn't matter. 19. He is learning to work rapidly. 20. Well, one has to work in order to eat.

Lección Once[1]

IDIOMS

¿cómo se llama? what is his name?

se llama (Juan), his name is (John)

otra cosa, something (anything) else

otra vez, again

ponerse a (trabajar), to begin (to work)

Mi vecino se llama Juan López. Aunque don Juan es viejo, goza de muy buena salud. Se levanta a las cinco y media de la mañana. Doña Ana se levanta a las cinco. Mientras don Juan se viste, doña Ana pone en la mesa café y pan duro. Nunca toman otra cosa por la mañana. Don Juan trabaja en los campos desde las siete hasta la una. Entonces se sienta debajo de un árbol. Después de comer se pone a trabajar otra vez. Por la noche, antes de acostarse, don Juan lee un libro. Se acuesta a las diez.

— ¿A qué hora se levanta Vd., María?

— Me levanto a las siete y cuarto.

— ¿Qué hace Vd. por la mañana?

— Hago muchas cosas. Ayudo a mi madre.

— Su hermano ayuda a su padre, ¿no es verdad?

— No, señor, mi hermano no trabaja nunca. Se levanta tarde, toma café, y se va.

---

[1] Above tenth, the cardinal numbers are generally used instead of the ordinal.

53. Reflexive Pronouns

me,	*myself*	nos,	*ourselves*
te,	*yourself* (tam.)	os,	*yourselves* (fam.)
se,	*yourself*	se,	*yourselves*
se,	*himself, herself, oneself*	se,	*themselves*

54. Reflexive Verbs

A reflexive verb has an object pronoun (reflexive) that refers back to the subject. The reflexive pronoun may be either direct or indirect object. It is indirect when the verb has another word as direct object.

DIRECT OBJECT:	**Juan se viste.**	*John dresses himself.*
INDIRECT OBJECT:	**Pepe se escribe una carta.**	*Joe writes a letter to himself.*

The reflexive form of the verb often has a different meaning. The following are important examples.

llamar,	*to call*	llamarse,	*to be called; to be named*
poner,	*to put, place*	ponerse,	*to put on*
acostar,	*to put to bed*	acostarse,	*to go to bed*
levantar,	*to raise, lift*	levantarse,	*to rise, get up*
sentar,	*to seat*	sentarse,	*to sit down*
ir,	*to go*	irse,	*to go away*

55. Present Indicative of *sentarse, to sit down*

me siento,	*I sit down*	nos sentamos,	*we sit down*
te sientas,	*you sit down*	os sentáis,	*you sit down*
se sienta,	*he sits down*	se sientan,	*they sit down*

56. Reciprocal Use of the Reflexive Pronoun

The reflexive pronoun may have reciprocal meaning. When necessary, ambiguity may be avoided by adding **uno a otro** (**una a otra**, etc.).

María y Ana se escriben.	*Mary and Anna write to each other.*
Estos niños se engañan uno a otro.	*These boys are deceiving each other.*

57. Time of Day

Time of day is expressed by the article **la** (**las**) plus the numeral. The article agrees with **hora** or **horas,** understood. The word for minute, generally omitted, is **minuto.**

¿Qué hora es?	*What time is it?*
¿A qué hora?	*At what time? when?*
Es la una.	*It is one o'clock.*
Son las dos.	*It is two o'clock.*
Son las nueve y cinco.	*It is five minutes past nine.*
Son las tres y cuarto.	*It is a quarter past three.*
A las ocho y media.	*At half past eight.*
A las once menos cuarto.	*At a quarter to eleven.*
A las siete de la mañana.	*At seven in the morning (A.M.).*
A las cinco de la tarde.	*At five in the afternoon (P.M.).*
A las diez de la noche.	*At ten in the evening (P.M.).*

de is used for English *in* when the hour is mentioned.

las cuatro de la tarde *four o'clock in the afternoon*

por is used when the hour is not mentioned.

por la tarde	*in the afternoon*
por la noche	*at night*

58. Present Indicative of *hacer* and *poner*

hacer, *to do, make*		poner, *to put, place*	
hago	hacemos	pongo	ponemos
haces	hacéis	pones	ponéis
hace	hacen	pone	ponen

Exercises

A. *Answer in Spanish.* 1. ¿Cómo se llama Vd.? 2. ¿Cómo se llama el vecino del autor? 3. ¿Goza Vd. de buena salud? 4. ¿A qué hora se levanta el señor López? 5. ¿A qué hora se levanta Vd.? 6. ¿A qué hora se levanta doña Ana? 7. Mientras don Juan se viste, ¿qué hace ella? 8. ¿Qué toman los dos todas las mañanas? 9. ¿No toman otra cosa? 10. ¿Dónde trabaja don Juan? 11. ¿Cuántas horas trabaja por la mañana? 12. ¿Qué hace don Juan a la una? 13. ¿Qué hace después de comer? 14. ¿Qué hace don Juan antes de acostarse? 15. ¿A qué hora se acuesta? 16. ¿A qué hora se acuesta Vd.?

B. *Copy the first paragraph of today's lesson, changing all verbs to the imperfect tense.*

C. *Answer affirmatively.* (*Model:* ¿Se levantan Vds.? Sí, señor, nos levantamos.) 1. ¿Se levanta Vd.? 2. ¿Me levanto yo? 3. ¿Se levantan ellos? 4. ¿Se acuesta Vd. tarde? 5. ¿Se acuestan Vds. tarde? *Answer negatively* (No, señor, *etc.*). 6. ¿Me siento? 7. ¿Se sienta Vd.? 8. ¿Nos sentamos? 9. ¿Se sientan Vds.? 10. ¿Se llama Vd. Juan? 11. ¿Se va Vd. a la una?

D. *Translate.* 1. At what time do you (*pl.*) eat? 2. We eat at half past eight. 3. When the teacher enters the classroom, we rise. 4. Can you tell me what time it is, John? 5. It is twenty minutes past nine. 6. I leave for Buenos Aires tomorrow at five minutes to three. 7. I have to get up at six o'clock in the morning. 8. Why are you putting on those things? 9. I am putting them on because I haven't anything else. 10. After dressing (myself), I am going to call my friend. 11. What is your friend's name? 12. His name is José, but I call him Pepe. 13. Does your father enjoy good health, John? 14. Yes, sir, but he no longer works in the afternoon. 15. He begins to work at seven thirty and finishes at twelve. 16. Sometimes he reads until eleven o'clock at night. 17. Although he goes to bed late, he gets up at five thirty. 18. While my father is dressing, I make the coffee. 19. Do you always eat stale bread? 20. No, sir, I never eat it. 21. Do you talk to each other while you are eating? 22. Of course, and sometimes we speak to each other in Spanish.

Vocabulary

NOUNS

la cosa, thing

don (*f.*, doña), *title equivalent to Mr.* (*Mrs.*), *but used only before the first name. Do not translate.*

la hora, hour; time (of day)

la mañana, morning; *adv.*, tomorrow

el minuto, minute

la noche, night

la salud, health

la tarde, afternoon; *adv.*, late

poner, to put, place

sentar (ie), to seat

vestir (i), to dress

ADVERBS

después, afterward

menos, less; except

mientras, while

PREPOSITIONS

después de, after

hasta, until

ADJECTIVES

duro -a, hard; pan duro, stale bread; *noun*, dollar

medio -a, half; media hora, half an hour

CONJUNCTION

aunque, although

OPTIONAL VOCABULARY

el sombrero, hat

el traje, suit (of clothes)

el zapato, shoe

me pongo el sombrero, I put on my hat

VERBS

acostar (ue), to put to bed

hacer, to do, make

levantar, to raise, lift

llamar, to call; to knock (*at the door*)

Refrán

Acostarse temprano y levantarse temprano, hace al hombre activo, rico y sano.

Early to bed and early to rise makes a man healthy, wealthy, and wise (*lit.*, . . . active, rich, and healthy).

Lección Doce

IDIOMS

al principio, at first
aquí lo tiene Vd., here it is
buenos días, good morning
llamar a la puerta, to knock (at the door)
sin embargo, nevertheless

Eran las once de la mañana cuando María salió de su casa.
Fué a casa de Ana. Subió a su cuarto, y llamó a la puerta.

ANA: Buenos días, María. ¿Cómo está Vd.?

MARÍA: Estoy bien, gracias. Vengo a traerle estas flores y a
enseñarle un vestido nuevo que compré ayer por la tarde. Aquí
lo tiene Vd. ¿Le gusta?

ANA: Me gusta mucho. ¿Dónde lo compró Vd.?

MARÍA: Lo compré en casa de García y Compañía. Es una
casa española, de modo que allí hay que hablar español. Creo
que al principio no me comprendieron. Sin embargo, al fin salí
con el vestido.

ANA: ¿Tenían otro igual?

MARÍA: Igual no, pero había uno muy semejante. Si Vd. quiere
comprar un vestido, debe ir a verlo.

ANA: ¿Cuánto vale?

MARÍA: Vale diecinueve pesos.

ANA: Pues, voy a verlo esta tarde. Tengo veinte pesos que

62

mi padre me dió para un vestido nuevo. Iba a comprarlo ayer por la mañana, pero me faltó tiempo.

59. The Preterit Indicative of Regular Verbs

The preterit has two sets of endings, one for -ar verbs (é, aste, ó, amos, asteis, aron) and one for -er and -ir verbs (í, iste, ió, imos, isteis, ieron). The preterit is translated like the English past tense: hablé, *I spoke, I did speak.*

hablar		comer		vivir	
hablé	hablamos	comí	comimos	viví	vivimos
hablaste	hablasteis	comiste	comisteis	viviste	vivisteis
habló	hablaron	comió	comieron	vivió	vivieron

60. Irregular Preterit of *dar*, *ser*, and *ir*

Note that **dar** has no written accent in the first person singular, and that the preterit of **ser** and **ir** is the same.

dar		ser		ir	
di	dimos	fuí	fuimos	fuí	fuimos
diste	disteis	fuiste	fuisteis	fuiste	fuisteis
dió	dieron	fué	fueron	fué	fueron

61. Uses of the Preterit

The preterit is the tense of narration. It corresponds, in general, to the English simple past tense. It stresses the completion of past acts or states. It is used

(a) to record a definitely terminated past act, or merely to state a fact.

María subió a su cuarto.	*Mary went up to her room.*
Llamó a la puerta.	*She knocked at the door.*
Vivió en España dos años.	*He lived in Spain for two years.*

(b) to record a series of past acts, if the series is taken as a completed whole.

Me engañó dos veces.	*He deceived me twice.*
Aquel año, se vieron todos los días.	*That year they saw each other every day.*

62. The Intransitive Verbs *gustar, faltar,* and *parecer*

Certain intransitive verbs are always used with an indirect object. The most important are **gustar,** *to be pleasing to;* **faltar,** *to be lacking;* and **parecer,** *to appear, seem; to think.*

Me gusta el vestido.	*I like the dress (The dress is pleasing to me).*
¿Le gustan a Vd. estas flores?	*Do you like these flowers?*
Me faltó tiempo para hacerlo.	*I didn't have time to do it (Time was lacking to me . . .).*
¿Qué les falta a Vds.?	*What do you lack?*
Nos faltan caballos.	*We lack horses.*
Me parece que tienen otro.	*I think (It seems to me) that they have another.*
A Juan le [1] parecía muy bonita.	*To John she seemed very pretty.*

63. Present Indicative of *traer* and *valer*

traer, *to bring*			valer, *to be worth*	
traigo	traemos		valgo	valemos
traes	traéis		vales	valéis
trae	traen		vale	valen

---

[1] Lit., *To John to him she seemed* . . . When a noun object precedes the verb, the redundant construction is used.

Exercises

A. *Answer in Spanish.* 1. ¿Qué hora era cuando María salió? 2. ¿Adónde fué María? 3. ¿Dónde estaba Ana cuando María subió a su cuarto? 4. ¿Quién llamó a la puerta? 5. Al entrar María, ¿qué le dice Ana? 6. ¿Qué trae María? 7. ¿Le gustan a Ana las flores? 8. ¿Le gusta el vestido? 9. ¿Es nuevo o viejo el vestido? 10. ¿Cuándo lo compró María? 11. ¿Lo compró en casa de Wanamaker? 12. ¿Es inglesa la casa de García y Compañía? 13. ¿Por qué entró María en esta casa? 14. ¿Qué cree María? 15. ¿Qué quiere saber Ana? 16. ¿Le parece a Vd. que Ana debe comprar el vestido? 17. ¿Cuánto vale el vestido? 18. ¿Cuánto dinero tiene Ana? 19. ¿Qué iba a comprar ayer por la mañana? 20. ¿Por qué no lo compró?

B. *The following forms are present indicative. Give the corresponding forms of the imperfect and preterit indicative.* (*Model:* **tomo,** *I take;* **tomaba,** *I was taking;* **tomé,** *I took*) 1. compro 2. bebo 3. escribo 4. doy 5. soy 6. voy 7. compra 8. Vd. bebe 9. Vds. escriben 10. damos 11. es 12. van

C. *Translate.* 1. Good morning, Mr. García. How are you? 2. Do you like the things that I bring you? 3. This dress does not seem new to me. 4. You are mistaken (deceiving yourself). 5. My sister has just bought one like it (**uno semejante**). 6. She is going to put it on now. 7. At first she did not like it. 8. You should not go away without seeing it. 9. But didn't I see it yesterday? 10. I was at Wanamaker's when your sister came in. 11. So you gave her the book? 12. Yes, I gave it to her yesterday afternoon. 13. How much are these flowers worth, Mr. López? 14. They are worth five dollars and a half. 15. If you want all the flowers, I can give them to you for (**por**) less. 16. I already owe you seven dollars and a half. 17. I don't know whether I ought to buy all these flowers. 18. Yesterday I went to my mother's room to ask her for money. 19. I knocked on the door before entering. 20. I don't wish to waste time. 21. Nevertheless, I still lack two things. 22. Do these dresses seem alike to you?

Vocabulary

NOUNS

la compañía, company
el embargo: sin embargo, nevertheless
la flor, flower
la gracia, grace; *pl.*, thanks
el peso, weight; dollar
el principio, beginning
el tiempo, time; weather
el vestido, dress

faltar, to lack, be lacking
gustar, to be pleasing to; to like
parecer, to appear, seem; to think
subir, to go up
traer, to bring
valer, to be worth

ADVERB

ayer, yesterday

ADJECTIVES

igual, equal, same; like, alike
nuevo -a, new
semejante, similar, alike

CONJUNCTION

si, if; whether

OPTIONAL VOCABULARY

el jardín, (flower) garden
la rosa, rose
    vender, to sell

VERBS

comprar, to buy
creer, to believe, think
deber, to owe; ought to, should

Refrán

Más vale tarde que nunca.
Better late than never.

Lección Trece

IDIOMS

a veces, at times
(dos pesos) al día, (two dollars) a (per) day
llegar a, to arrive in
me quedan dos pesos, I have two dollars left (two dollars remain to me)
no me quedan más que dos pesos, I have only two dollars left
tratar de (engañar), to try (to deceive)

JUAN: ¿Cuántos años estuvo Vd. en Buenos Aires, Paco?

PACO: Estuve allí cuatro años y medio.

JUAN: ¿Le gustó esa ciudad?

PACO: Al principio, no. Al llegar a Buenos Aires, no me quedaban más que dieciocho pesos. Tuve que buscar trabajo. Anduve por las calles de la ciudad cinco días enteros, antes de colocarme. Al fin, me dió trabajo don Juan Pacheco. Por la mañana tenía que escribir cartas en español y en inglés. Escribía más de veinte cartas cada mañana. A veces me ayudaban los hijos del señor Pacheco. Empezábamos a las ocho de la mañana. Por la tarde, yo conducía el automóvil. Llevaba a don Juan a todas partes. Algunas veces le llevaba a un lugar fuera de la ciudad, donde compraba vino y otras cosas. Don Juan y sus hijos me trataban muy bien. Ahora, don Juan me parece el hombre más bueno del mundo y Buenos Aires la ciudad más hermosa del mundo. ¿La conoce Vd., Juan?

67

South America

(La América del Sur)

Argentina (pop. 12,561,361):[1] capital, Buenos Aires. Chief exports: meats, wheat and flour, linseed, maize, wool, hides, dairy products, cotton, quebracho extract.

Bolivia (pop. 3,266,296): capital, La Paz. Chief exports: tin, lead, copper, silver, rubber.

Brazil (pop. 45,332,660): capital, Río de Janeiro. Chief exports: coffee, cotton, cattle hides, cacao, meats, oil seeds and kernels, mate, tobacco, lumber, rubber.

Chile (pop. 4,626,508): capital, Santiago. Chief exports: nitrate, copper, iodine, wool, meat, hides and skins, iron ore, gold.

Colombia (pop. 8,698,634): capital, Bogotá. Chief exports: coffee, bananas, hides and skins, petroleum, platinum, gold.

Ecuador (pop. 2,756,552): capital, Quito. Chief exports: ivory nuts, petroleum, cacao, straw hats, coffee, gold, silver, rice, rubber, bananas.

Paraguay (pop. 931,799): capital, Asunción. Chief exports: quebracho extract, mate, cotton, tobacco, cattle hides, beef extract.

Peru (pop. 6,500,000): capital, Lima. Chief exports: cotton, sugar, copper, petroleum, wool, balata, hides and skins, bismuth.

Uruguay (pop. 2,065,986): capital, Montevideo. Chief exports: beef, cattle hides, wool, linseed, canned meats, sand.

Venezuela (pop. 3,451,677): capital, Caracas. Chief exports: coffee, cacao, hides and skins, petroleum, pearls.

South America has three great river systems:

(1) The Amazon River (**el río Amazonas**) is navigable for a distance of 2,300 miles for ocean-going vessels. It has approximately 200 tributaries, forming the world's largest river system, with about 30,000 miles of navigable waters.

(2) The La Plata system, formed by the Paraná, the Paraguay, and the Uruguay, drains one of the most productive regions of South America. The La Plata itself (*el río de la Plata*), between Argentina and Uruguay, is really not a river, but an estuary. It is 185 miles long and about 145 miles wide at its mouth.

(3) The Orinoco and its tributaries form the third great river system. Small boats can pass from the Orinoco to the Amazon, since the Casiquiare, a branch of the Orinoco, connects with the Rio Negro, a tributary of the Amazon.

An airplane flying straight south from New York would pass over the western coast of South America.

Brazil is larger than the United States (exclusive of Alaska) by 250,000 square miles or by an area almost as large as Texas.

The Amazon basin has 20,000 species of hardwoods.

About two thirds of the world's supply of coffee is produced in Brazil.

India was the only source of diamonds until 1728, when they were discovered in Brazil. Brazil is still an important source of these precious stones, though the chief supply now comes from South Africa, where they were discovered in 1876.

---

[1] All population figures are from *The World Almanac* for 1939.

Among the mineral resources of Brazil, iron is by far the most important. The deposits in Minas Geraes alone are estimated to contain 12,000,000,000 tons of high-grade ore.

The highest peak of the western hemisphere is Mt. Aconcagua (23,094 feet) in Chile.

In January, 1939, an earthquake devastated the six southern provinces of Chile, destroying a score of cities, among them Concepción and Chillán, where scarcely a building was left standing. About 30,000 lives were lost. From 1907 to 1924 there were 12,694 earthquakes in Chile, an average of two a day.

Lake Titicaca, in the Andes Mountains between Bolivia and Peru, is the highest (12,600 feet) body of navigable water in the world. It is approximately as large as the state of Connecticut.

The highest city in the world is Potosí (14,350 feet) in Bolivia, second largest producer of tin. The tin and silver mines of Potosí are so high that only natives, long accustomed to the rarified atmosphere, can work in them.

The "Irish" potato, the tomato, the bean (both lima and navy), and tobacco are all native to South America. The potato was widely cultivated from Chile to Colombia at the period of the Spanish conquest. The tomato, formerly called the love apple and regarded as poisonous, was found by the Spaniards in Peru. Here also were found the first tobacco plants. Tobacco was introduced into France in 1559 by Jean Nicot, whence the term *nicotine*.

The oldest university in the western hemisphere, San Marcos at Lima, Peru, was founded in 1551. Harvard University, oldest in the United States, was founded in 1636.

Colombia is the world's principal source of emeralds.

Buenos Aires has the largest refrigerating plant in the world, with a daily capacity of 5,000 cattle and 10,000 sheep.

JUAN: No, señor, no la conozco. Espero conocerla, sin embargo, dentro de algunos años. Espero conocer también a don Juan Pacheco. Ahora, no tengo bastante dinero para un viaje tan largo. No gano más que cinco pesos al día.

PACO: Pues Vd. gana más que yo. Yo no tengo trabajo.

64. Comparison of Adjectives.

The comparative and superlative degrees are both formed by placing **más** before the adjective.

POSITIVE		COMPARATIVE AND SUPERLATIVE	
rico,	*rich*	**más rico,**	*richer, richest*
triste,	*sad*	**más triste,**	*sadder, saddest*
hermoso,	*beautiful*	**más hermoso,**	*more beautiful, most beautiful*

All adjectives are compared as above, but the following adjectives may also be compared irregularly.

bueno,	*good*	**mejor,**	*better, best*
malo,	*bad*	**peor,**	*worse, worst*
grande,	*large*	**mayor,**	*larger, largest* [1]
pequeño,	*small*	**menor,**	*smaller, smallest* [1]

65. Comparison of Adverbs

Adverbs are compared like adjectives.

lejos, far   **más lejos,** *farther, farthest*

The following adverbs are compared irregularly.

mucho,	*much*	**más,**	*more, most*
poco,	*little*	**menos,**	*less, least*
bien,	*well*	**mejor,**	*better, best*
mal,	*badly*	**peor,**	*worse, worst*

66. que, *than*

than is regularly translated by **que.** Before a number, **de** must be used.

---

[1] Referring to persons, **mayor** may mean *older, oldest* and **menor,** *younger, youngest.*

Juan tiene más libros que María.	*John has more books than Mary.*
Escribió más de veinte cartas.	*He wrote more than twenty letters.*

Keep in mind that

1. **no . . . más que** usually means *only*.

No escribió más que veinte.	*He wrote only twenty.*
No gano más que cinco pesos al día.	*I earn only five dollars per day.*

2. *in* after a superlative is translated by **de**.

Es la ciudad más hermosa del mundo.	*It is the most beautiful city in the world.*
Es el muchacho más alto de la clase.	*He is the tallest boy in the class.*

67. Present Indicative of *conocer* and *conducir*

Verbs like **parecer, conocer,** and **conducir,** i.e., ending in a vowel + **cer** or **cir,** have **-zco** in the first person singular. See § 132, No. 8, and § 135.

conocer, *to know*[1] (*be acquainted with*); *to meet*		conducir, *to lead, conduct;* *to drive* (a car)	
conozco	conocemos	conduzco	conducimos
conoces	conocéis	conduces	conducís
conoce	conocen	conduce	conducen

68. Preterit of *andar, estar,* and *tener*

andar	estar	tener
anduve	estuve	tuve
anduviste	estuviste	tuviste
anduvo	estuvo	tuvo
anduvimos	estuvimos	tuvimos
anduvisteis	estuvisteis	tuvisteis
anduvieron	estuvieron	tuvieron

---

[1] Note carefully the difference in meaning between **saber,** *to know* (*have information concerning; know how to; find out*) and **conocer,** *to know* (*be acquainted with persons or things; to meet, make the acquaintance of*).

Exercises

A. *Answer in Spanish.* 1. ¿Cuántos años estuvo Paco en Buenos Aires? 2. ¿Cuántos pesos le quedaban al llegar a Buenos Aires? 3. ¿Qué tuvo que hacer? 4. ¿Cuántos días anduvo por las calles antes de colocarse? 5. Al fin, ¿quién le dió trabajo? 6. ¿Qué tenía que hacer por la mañana? 7. ¿Cuántas cartas escribía cada mañana? 8. ¿Quién le ayudaba a veces? 9. ¿A qué hora empezaban a trabajar? 10. ¿Qué hacía Paco por la tarde? 11. ¿Adónde llevaba a don Juan? 12. ¿Adónde le llevaba para comprar vino? 13. ¿Cómo trataban a Paco los hijos de don Juan? 14. A Paco, ¿quién le parece el hombre más bueno del mundo? 15. ¿Qué ciudad le parece la más hermosa del mundo? 16. ¿Por qué no va Juan a Buenos Aires? 17. ¿Espera Vd. ir a Buenos Aires dentro de algunos años? 18. ¿Cuánto gana Juan cada día? 19. ¿Gana más o menos que Paco? 20. ¿Quién no tiene trabajo?

B. *Read aloud, translating the italicized words.* 1. Juan es *taller than* Pepe. 2. Esta agua está *colder than* aquélla. 3. Aquellos niños son *smaller than* éstos. 4. María es la niña *prettiest in* la clase. 5. Estuvieron en Méjico *more than* siete años. 6. Estas casas son *older than* aquéllas. 7. El señor García es el hombre *richest in the* pueblo. 8. Este vino es *better than* aquél. 9. Ana es *older than* su hermano. 10. Habla español *worse than* yo.

C. *Write the corresponding forms of the imperfect and preterit.* 1. estoy 2. está 3. colocan 4. andamos 5. conozco 6. empieza 7. tiene 8. quedo 9. esperamos 10. trata

D. *Translate.* 1. Mr. García's automobile doesn't run well. 2. It ran very well yesterday. 3. How long (¿**Cuánto tiempo**) did Frank stay in Buenos Aires? 4. At first he didn't like the city. 5. Finally the house of Pacheco and Company gave him work. 6. He had only two dollars left. 7. They tried to place me, but there was no work. 8. John hopes to get a job (place himself) in another city. 9. How much money do you (*pl.*) have

left?   10. Each one (**A cada uno le**) has fifteen dollars left.
11. We haven't enough money for a long trip.   12. You (*pl.*)
should wait until tomorrow.   13. Within a few days I hope to
make the trip.   14. My uncle and aunt spent a whole year in that
place.   15. Do you know the man that is driving the automobile?
16. Yes, I met him in Buenos Aires.   17. I think he is waiting for
you.   18. At times it seems to me that he is trying to deceive me.
19. Will you tell me whether Mr. Pacheco arrived in New York
yesterday?   20. I have just seen him. He expects to remain here
more than ten days.   21. Some of his friends are coming later.
22. Who is the richest man in the world?

Vocabulary

NOUNS

el **automóvil**, automobile
el **hombre**, man
el **lugar**, place; village
el **mundo**, world
Paco, Frank
el **trabajo**, work
el **viaje**, trip, voyage

ADJECTIVES

bastante, enough
cada, each, every
entero -a, entire, whole
largo -a, long

VERBS

andar, to go, run (*of a machine*);
  to walk
colocar, to place; **colocarse**, to get
  a job (place oneself)
conducir, to lead, conduct; **to**
  drive (*a car*)

conocer, to know; to meet
empezar (ie), to begin
esperar, to hope, expect; to wait
  for
ganar, to gain, earn
llegar, to arrive
quedar, to remain, be left, stay;
  quedarse, to stay
tratar (de), to treat; to try

ADVERB

dentro, inside; *prep.*, **dentro de,**
  within

OPTIONAL VOCABULARY

el **coche**, car, cab
corto -a, short

Y es que en el mundo traidor
Nada hay verdad ni mentira:
Todo es según el color
Del cristal con que se mira.[1]

And the fact is that in this deceitful world there is nothing true nor false: everything is according to the color of the glass with which one views it.

---

[1] From *Las dos linternas* by Ramón de Campoamor (1817–1901).

Lección Catorce

IDIOMS

en cuanto a, as for; concerning
haber de, to be to; han de salir, they are to leave
la mayor parte de, most of
(responder) que sí (que no), (to answer) yes (no)

Méjico, 2 de abril de 1938

Querido Luis:

Siento decirle que no he hallado todavía la obra de López y Fuentes [1] que Vd. me pide en su última carta. Espero poder mandársela, sin embargo, dentro de algunos días. Antes de recibir su carta, ya le había mandado algunas vistas de la Ciudad de Méjico. Hoy le mando otras.

En cuanto a los objetos de arte, pienso comprarlos mañana. ¿Le mando la cuenta a Vd., o a su padre?

En cuanto a la orden del señor White, pregunté a mi padre si la había recibido. Respondió que sí. Añadió que ya estaban en camino la mayor parte de los libros. Los demás han de salir mañana. Tuvimos que pedirlos a una casa de Barcelona.

Recuerdos a todos. Como siempre, su amigo,

Carlos Vargas

---

[1] In Spanish-speaking countries the mother's maiden name is often added to the family name of the father. The y is frequently omitted. Gregorio López y Fuentes is a Mexican novelist (1896–   ), author of *El indio* and other novels of the Mexican revolution.

69. The Past Participle

The past participle of regular verbs is formed by adding **-ado** to the stem of **-ar** verbs and **-ido** to the stem of **-er** and **-ir** verbs.

hablar, *to speak*	**hablado,** *spoken*
comer, *to eat*	**comido,** *eaten*
vivir, *to live*	**vivido,** *lived*

70. Irregular Past Participles

The following verbs have irregular past participles.

(decir)	**dicho,** *said, told*		(abrir)	**abierto,** *opened, open*
(hacer)	**hecho,** *done, made*		(cubrir)	**cubierto,** *covered*
(poner)	**puesto,** *put, placed*		(volver)	**vuelto,** *returned*
(ver)	**visto,** *seen*		(morir)	**muerto,** *died, dead*
(escribir)	**escrito,** *written*			

Note that the regular participial ending **-ido** requires a written accent, if the stem of the verb ends in a strong vowel.

(creer)	**creído**	(leer)	**leído**
(traer)	**traído**	(oír)	**oído**

71. The Auxiliary Verb *haber,* to have

PRESENT		IMPERFECT	
he	hemos	había	habíamos
has	habéis	habías	habíais
ha	han	había	habían

72. Compound Tenses

The present perfect indicative is formed with the present tense of **haber,** *to have,* and a past participle. The past perfect indicative is formed with the imperfect tense of **haber** and a past participle. With **haber,** the past participle is invariable (always ends in **-o**).

PRESENT PERFECT INDICATIVE	PAST PERFECT INDICATIVE
he hablado (comido, vivido)	había hablado (comido, vivido)
has hablado	habías hablado
ha hablado	había hablado
hemos hablado	habíamos hablado
habéis hablado	habíais hablado
han hablado	habían hablado

Translation: he hablado (comido, vivido), *I have spoken (eaten, lived)*, etc.

habla había hablado (comido, vivido), *I had spoken (eaten, lived)*, etc.

73. Uses of the Perfect Tenses

In general, the present perfect and the past perfect (pluperfect) are used as in English.

No he hallado la obra.	*I have not found the work.*
¿Ha comido Vd. la carne?	*Have you eaten the meat?*
Hemos escrito dos cartas.	*We have written two letters.*
Ya les había mandado las vistas.	*I had already sent them the views.*
No las habían recibido.	*They had not received them.*

Note, however, that the present perfect may be used for the English past to express an act closely related to the present.

¿Qué ha dicho Vd.? *What did you say?*

74. The Expression *haber de*

English *am to*, *is to*, etc., indicating future time or obligation, is translated by **haber de** + the infinitive.

Han de salir mañana.	*They are to leave tomorrow.*
¿Qué ha de hacer?	*What is he to do* (under the circumstances)?

75. Indirect Object after *preguntar, pedir,* and *comprar*

After **preguntar,** *to ask (inquire),* **pedir,** *to ask for, order,* and **comprar,** *to buy,* the person involved is always *indirect object.*

Pregunté a mi padre si la había recibido.	*I asked my father whether he had received it.*
He pedido el libro al señor Vargas.	*I have ordered the book from Mr. Vargas.*
Compré las vistas a Carlos.	*I bought the views from Charles.*

Exercises

A. *Answer in Spanish.* 1. Antes de escribir a Luis, ¿qué había buscado Carlos? 2. ¿En qué carta había pedido Luis la obra? 3. ¿Qué le había mandado Carlos? 4. ¿Qué clase de objetos había pedido Luis? 5. ¿Cuándo pensaba Carlos mandárselos? 6. En cuanto a la cuenta, ¿qué quería saber Carlos? 7. En cuanto a la orden del señor White, ¿qué preguntó Carlos a su padre? 8. ¿Cómo respondió el señor Vargas? 9. ¿Qué añadió? 10. ¿Han de salir hoy los demás libros? 11. ¿A qué casa tuvo que pedirlos el señor Vargas? 12. ¿Cómo termina la carta?

B. *Translate orally.* 1. What did you say? 2. What have they done? 3. Where have you put it? 4. Have you (*pl.*) seen him? 5. We have written to them. 6. I had not opened it (*f.*). 7. They had covered the table. 8. We had not returned. 9. The horses had died. 10. I had not read the letter.

C. *Translate.* 1. Are you acquainted with the art of Mexico? 2. I am sorry to say that I do not know it well. 3. My father tells me that there are beautiful views on the road that leads to Mexico City. 4. It is true. I have seen them many times. 5. Have those objects of Spanish art arrived? [1] 6. Not yet. I always order them from a Barcelona house. 7. They have already found most of the pictures. 8. As for the rest, they intend to send them within

---

[1] **¿Han llegado** . . . Do not separate the auxiliary from the past participle.

a few days. 9. Mr. Vargas, did you ask Charles whether he had received my letter? 10. I did not ask him (**No se lo**) [1] because he had not returned. 11. Have you read the last work of Blasco Ibáñez? 12. I have looked for it, but I haven't found it. 13. Who is to tell the general that his son has died? 14. I don't know who it is to be. 15. Can you tell me why they have added five dollars to my bill? 16. I asked Mr. Vargas. 17. He replied that he had not seen the order. 18. Dear Mary: Why haven't you written to me? 19. You haven't told me whether you received the flowers. 20. Will you open that letter? 21. I have already opened it. 22. In it he says: "Regards to all my friends."

Vocabulary

NOUNS

abril, April
el arte,[2] art
el camino, road
la cuenta, bill
el objeto, object
la obra, work (e.g., *a book*)
la orden, order
el recuerdo, remembrance; *pl.*, regards
la vista, view

VERBS

abrir, to open
añadir, to add
hallar, to find
mandar, to command, order; to send
pensar (ie), to think; to intend
preguntar, to ask, inquire
recibir, to receive
responder, to reply, answer
sentir (ie), to regret; to feel

ADJECTIVES

demás: *adj. & pro.*, los demás, the others, the rest
querido -a, dear
último -a, last

ADVERB

siempre, always

---

[1] See note 1, p. 48.
[2] arte may be either masculine or feminine. In most cases it is feminine, especially when used in the plural. See note 1, p. 13.

OPTIONAL VOCABULARY

Los meses del año

enero,	January	julio,	July
febrero,	February	agosto,	August
marzo,	March	septiembre,[1]	September
abril,	April	octubre,	October
mayo,	May	noviembre,	November
junio,	June	diciembre,	December

Refrán

Piensa el ladrón que todos son de su condición.
The thief thinks that everyone is a thief.

---

[1] Pronounced (and often spelled) **setiembre.**

Lección Quince

IDIOMS

a pesar de, in spite of
darse cuenta de, to realize
dolor de cabeza, headache
hace (un mes), (a month) ago
ponerse (malo), to become (ill)
¿Qué tiene (Luis)? What is the matter with (Louis)?
tener razón, to be right; **no tener razón,** to be wrong
todo el mundo, everybody

— Dígame, Luis, ¿durmió Vd. bien anoche?

— Apenas cerré los ojos. No pude dormir. ¿Y usted?

— ¿Yo? Siempre duermo bien. Me doy cuenta de que el sueño es cosa muy necesaria. El hombre es animal y las leyes de la naturaleza le obligan a dormir. Vd. va a ponerse malo, porque ni duerme ni come.

— En cuanto a esas leyes, tiene Vd. razón, pero el hombre puede pasar varios días sin dormir, a pesar de todas las leyes de la naturaleza.

— Sí, es verdad, pero, ¿por qué no pudo Vd. dormir? Ya sabe Vd. que no hay efecto sin causa. Al acostarse me dijo que estaba muy cansado.

— La causa es la muerte de mi tío. Murió en Cuba hace un mes, pero no lo supe hasta ayer por la tarde. Era muy buena persona. Todo el mundo le amaba.

82

— Ahora comprendo por qué Vd. no quiso acompañarnos al teatro, Luis. Siéntese Vd. Tome este café y coma algo.

— Muy bien, démelo. Tengo dolor de cabeza.

76. Commands

The command form (with **usted, ustedes**) is found by taking the stem of the first person singular present indicative and adding

-e, -en (to the stem of **-ar** verbs)
-a, -an (to the stem of **-er** and **-ir** verbs)

	STEM	COMMAND FORM		
tomo	tom-	**tome (Vd.)**	**tomen (Vds.)**	*take*
como	com-	**coma (Vd.)**	**coman (Vds.)**	*eat*
pongo	pong-	**ponga (Vd.)**	**pongan (Vds.)**	*put*
digo	dig-	**diga (Vd.)**	**digan (Vds.)**	*say, tell*
vengo	veng-	**venga (Vd.)**	**vengan (Vds.)**	*come*
oigo	oig-	**oiga (Vd.)**	**oigan (Vds.)**	*listen*

The command form of **dar** is **dé** (*pl.*, **den**), of **ir**, **vaya** (*pl.*, **vayan**).

Object pronouns are attached to the command form when it is affirmative. They precede when it is negative. The written accent is required when a pronoun is attached to the verb.

Siéntese Vd., Luis.	*Sit down, Louis.*
No se siente Vd. aquí.	*Don't sit down here.*
Tome Vd. el café.	*Take the coffee.*
Déme la flor.[1]	*Give me the flower.*
No se la dé a ella.	*Do not give it to her.*
Vayan Vds. a casa.	*Go home.*

77. Uses of the Definite Article

The definite article is used (a) with nouns denoting a general class, and (b) with abstract nouns.

---

[1] The command form **dé** is accented, even when a pronoun is attached. The pronoun **Vd. (Vds.)** is frequently omitted in a command.

(a) **El hombre es animal.**   *Man is an animal.*
    Me gustan las flores.   *I like flowers.*
(b) **La muerte viene a todo el mundo.**   *Death comes to everybody.*
    Es una ley de la naturaleza.   *It is a law of nature.*

78. Preterit of Radical-Changing Verbs

The preterit of **-ar** and **-er** radical-changing verbs is regular.
-ir verbs change **e** to **i** and **o** to **u** in the third person, singular and
plural.

pedir		sentir		dormir	
pedí	pedimos	sentí	sentimos	dormí	dormimos
pediste	pedisteis	sentiste	sentisteis	dormiste	dormisteis
pidió	pidieron	sintió	sintieron	durmió	durmieron

79. Irregular Preterits

poner		decir	
puse	pusimos	dije	dijimos
pusiste	pusisteis	dijiste	dijisteis
puso	pusieron	dijo	dijeron

Preterits like **poner** are:

    hacer: hice, hiciste, hizo, hicimos, hicisteis, hicieron
    poder: pude, pudiste, etc.
    querer: quise, quisiste, etc.
    saber: supe, supiste, etc.[1]
    venir: vine, viniste, etc.

Preterits like **decir** are:

    conducir: conduje, condujiste, etc.
    traer: traje, trajiste, etc.

---

[1] In the preterit, **saber** means *learned of, found out:* **Supo que su tío había muerto.**
He learned that his uncle had died.

Exercises

A. *Answer in Spanish.* 1. ¿Qué le preguntó Juan a Luis?
2. ¿Qué respondió Luis? 3. ¿Quién siempre duerme bien?
4. ¿De qué se da cuenta Juan? 5. ¿Puede vivir el hombre sin
dormir? 6. ¿Qué leyes le obligan a dormir? 7. ¿Qué le pasa a una
persona, si no duerme ni come? 8. ¿Qué puede hacer un hombre,
a pesar de las leyes de la naturaleza? 9. ¿Qué dice Juan de causas
y efectos? 10. ¿Qué dijo Luis anoche, al acostarse? 11. ¿Cuándo
murió su tío? 12. ¿Cuándo lo supo Luis? 13. ¿Qué clase de
persona era su tío? 14. ¿Quién le amaba? 15. ¿Qué no quiso
hacer anoche Luis? 16. ¿Qué tiene Luis?

B. *Change the following to affirmative commands, singular and
plural.* (*Model:* comerlo — cómalo, cómanlo) 1. escribirlo
2. cerrar la puerta 3. decírmelo 4. dárselos a ella 5. ir a las
cinco 6. pedírselas a él 7. ponerla aquí 8. hacerlo mañana
9. traérnoslo 10. mandármelos

C. *Repeat exercise B, making the commands negative.*

D. *Write, with translations, the corresponding forms of the imperfect and preterit.* 1. pide 2. siente 3. duerme 4. pongo
5. hace 6. hago 7. quieren 8. saben 9. vienen 10. damos
11. soy 12. va 13. digo 14. traen

E. *Translate.* 1. Louis doesn't like wine. 2. Well then,
don't give it to him. 3. Last night, after drinking it, he had a
headache. 4. Later he became very ill. 5. He hardly slept half
an hour. 6. I realize that sleep is necessary. 7. As for that,
you are right. 8. Learn nature's laws, if you wish to enjoy good
health. 9. Louis's uncle died several days ago. 10. Did you
(*pl.*) find out the cause of his death? 11. They told me that he
wouldn't (**no quiso**) eat. 12. Finally they compelled him to eat
something. 13. In spite of this he became worse. 14. He lived
in the country because he loved nature. 15. Who is going to
accompany you to the theater? 16. The theater is closed, so we
are not going.

Vocabulary

NOUNS

la **cabeza**, head
la **causa**, cause
el **dolor**, pain
el **efecto**, effect
la **ley**, law
la **muerte**, death
la **naturaleza**, nature
la **persona**, person
la **razón**, reason
el **sueño**, sleep

PRONOUN

algo, something

ADJECTIVES

cansado -a, tired
necesario -a, necessary
vario -a, different; *pl.*, several

VERBS

acompañar, to accompany
amar, to love
cerrar (ie), to close
dormir (ue), to sleep
morir (ue), to die
obligar (a), to oblige, compel

ADVERBS

anoche, last night
apenas, hardly, scarcely

CONJUNCTION

ni, nor; **ni . . . ni**, neither . . . nor

OPTIONAL VOCABULARY

la **estación**, station; season (*of the year*)

LAS ESTACIONES DEL AÑO

la **primavera**, spring
el **verano**, summer
el **otoño**, autumn
el **invierno**, winter

De la pobreza, la industria;
de la industria, la riqueza;
de la riqueza, el orgullo;
del orgullo, la pobreza.

From poverty, industry;
from industry, wealth;
from wealth, pride;
from pride, poverty.

Repaso

A. *Copy, translating the italicized words.* 1. *I went to bed* a las once. 2. *I got up* a las siete y media. 3. *She put on* el vestido. 4. *They sat down* debajo de un árbol. 5. *I can dress* en cinco minutos. 6. Hoy, *I stay* en casa. 7. ¿*Did he go away* sin decirle a Vd. *what his name is?* 8. Los dos hermanos *love each other* mucho. 9. Estos hombres *do not treat themselves* mal. 10. *We see each other* todos los días.

B. *Change each of the following* (a) *to an affirmative command,* (b) *to a negative command.* 1. cerrar la ventana 2. abrirla 3. preguntárselo 4. mandárselos a ellos 5. empezar ahora 6. traérmelas 7. creerlo 8. comprarlo a Juan 9. vestirse 10. levantarse

C. *Translate.* 1. I gave it (*m.*) to her. 2. He gave them (*f.*) to me. 3. It was not he who did it. 4. We walked two hours that day. 5. You didn't have to do it. 6. He said he was in that place twenty minutes. 7. He asked me for it (*f.*). 8. I asked him if he had bought it (*m.*). 9. I regretted it and he regretted it too. 10. Did you put them (*m.*) there? 11. I couldn't do it then. 12. Who did it? 13. I did it later. 14. He tried (**querer**) to answer, but he couldn't. 15. How did you find it out? 16. John came to my house last night. 17. He led me to the place. 18. Who brought you the letter?

D. *Translate the italicized words.* 1. *He has not told me* la hora. 2. El hombre *had not returned* a casa. 3. Supe que *he had died.* 4. *He had made* un viaje muy largo. 5. *Have you covered* esas cosas? 6. ¿Quién *has opened* la carta? 7. *I hadn't read it.* 8. *We haven't seen it.*

E. *Translate the italicized words.* 1. Esta compañía *is better than* aquélla. 2. Ella tiene *more time than* nosotros. 3. Este objeto *is harder than* ése. 4. Aquellos hombres *are more tired than* éstos. 5. Hallé la cuenta hace *more than* dos horas. 6. Ganaba *less than* tres pesos al día. 7. Esta obra *is better than* aquélla. 8. Ésta *is the best* obra de Cervantes. 9. *He is the worst* muchacho *in* la clase. 10. Habla español *better than* yo.

F. *Translate.* 1. How many things do we lack? 2. It seems to me that all are here. 3. Well then, give them to him. 4. What is his name? 5. I don't know, although I met him last night. 6. Ask him if this is the road that we are to take. 7. He is to accompany us, so it isn't necessary. 8. John doesn't intend to go. 9. Yes, I know. He has a headache. 10. He went up to his room while we were talking. 11. He doesn't like long trips. 12. At first I didn't like them either. 13. Nevertheless, most men love nature. 14. You are right, but you should add something. 15. Some men do not love work. 16. Who knocked at the door a few minutes ago? 17. It was the person from whom you bought the last picture. 18. My dear Charles, do I have to tell you again that I did not buy it? 19. I tried to buy it, but I didn't have enough money left. 20. Now, I realize that it was hardly worth twenty dollars. 21. Good morning, Mr. Jones. I have brought you the flowers. 22. Do you wish anything else this morning? 23. No, thanks. In spite of the bad weather, I am leaving within half an hour. 24. Joe nearly always goes with me, but last night he became ill.

Lección Dieciséis

IDIOMS

con mucho gusto, gladly
en efecto, in fact, as a matter of fact
en primer lugar, in the first place
hacen falta (tales locos), (such madmen) are needed; **me hace falta** (dinero), I need (money)
hágame el favor de (decírmelo), please (tell me)
quiero decir, I mean
sobre todo, especially
vuelve a (leerlo), (he reads it) again

— Veo que Vd. ha comprado el *Quijote*, don Juan.

— No, Luis. Hace más de treinta años que tengo ese libro. Mi padre me lo trajo de España en el año 1908 (mil novecientos ocho). Cuando volvía de un viaje, me traía siempre un buen libro.

— Su padre tenía buen gusto. Según mi tío, ese libro es el mejor que ha salido de España.

— Pues a mí me parece el mejor del mundo. Lo he leído cinco veces, y pienso volver a leerlo otras cinco. ¿Lo conoce Vd., Luis?

— No, señor, yo no sé todavía bastante español para leer el *Quijote*. Sin embargo, espero leerlo algún día. Hágame Vd. el favor de decirme algo de este caballero loco.

— Con mucho gusto. En primer lugar, Vd. ha de saber que el

autor, Miguel de Cervantes, nació en 1547 (mil quinientos cuarenta y siete) y murió en 1616 (mil seiscientos dieciséis), el mismo año en que murió el gran autor inglés Shakespeare. Desde un punto de vista, aun vive Cervantes. Vive en sus obras, sobre todo en el *Quijote*. Y, en efecto, merece vida eterna. El caballero que nos presenta Cervantes es loco, como Vd. ha dicho. Pero este loco, según las palabras del gran poeta de Nicaragua (quiero decir Rubén Darío [1]), es "la vida y la naturaleza." Don Quijote es ejemplo de la virtud; y, como él mismo nos dice, quiere hacer bien a todos y mal a ninguno. Tales locos hacen falta en el mundo, Luis.

80. Shortened Forms of Adjectives

The following adjectives drop the -o before a masculine singular noun. Note the written accent on the shortened forms of **alguno** and **ninguno**.

bueno	un buen libro,	*a good book*
malo	mal gusto,	*bad taste*
primero	en primer lugar,	*in the first place*
tercero	el tercer ejemplo,	*the third example*
alguno	algún día,	*some day*
ninguno	ningún hombre,	*no man*

grande usually becomes **gran** before a noun of either gender. When used before a noun it generally means *great*.

> un gran autor español　　*a great Spanish author*

81. Time Expressions with *hacer*

(a) **hace**, *it makes*, is used for English *ago*.

> **Me lo trajo hace dos días,** or　　*He brought it to me two days*
> **Hace dos días que me lo trajo.**　　*ago* (lit., *it makes two days*).

---

[1] Rubén Darío (1867–1916), prince of the "modernist" poets. The quotation is from his beautiful sonnet to Cervantes.

(b) The *present* tense (with **hace**) is used in Spanish to indicate that an act or state, begun in the past, is still in progress.

Hace treinta años que lo tengo.	*I have had it for thirty years.*
Hace media hora que escribe.	*He has been writing for half an hour.*

(c) The *imperfect* tense (with **hacía**) is used when the progress of the act or state is interrupted before reaching the present.

Hacía dos años que estaba en Méjico, cuando murió su padre.	*He had been in Mexico for two years when his father died.*
Hacía un año que lo buscábamos.	*We had been looking for it for a year.*

Important: Keep in mind that in type (b) *both* verbs are in the *present* tense, and in type (c) *both* verbs are in the *imperfect* tense.

82. Cardinal Numbers (*continued*)

31	treinta y uno, etc.	400	cuatrocientos -as
40	cuarenta	500	quinientos -as
50	cincuenta	600	seiscientos -as
60	sesenta	700	setecientos -as
70	setenta	800	ochocientos -as
80	ochenta	900	novecientos -as
90	noventa	1,000	mil
100	ciento	2,000	dos mil
200	doscientos -as	1,000,000	un millón
300	trescientos -as	2,000,000	dos millones

ciento becomes **cien** before a noun or before a number that it multiplies.

cien cosas	*a hundred things*
cien mil hombres	*a hundred thousand men*
But: ciento siete	*a hundred (and) seven*

A multiple of **ciento** agrees with the noun to which it refers.

> **trescientos libros**   *three hundred books*
> **quinientas casas**   *five hundred houses*

un is not used before **ciento** nor before **mil**.

> **cien mesas**   *one hundred tables*
> **mil gracias**   *a thousand thanks*

millón is a noun and must be preceded by **un** and followed by **de**.

> **un millón de libros**   *a million books*

83. Ordinal Numbers

primero -a,	*first*	**sexto -a,**	*sixth*
segundo -a,	*second*	**séptimo -a,**	*seventh*
tercero -a,	*third*	**octavo -a,**	*eighth*
cuarto -a,	*fourth*	**noveno -a,**	*ninth*
quinto -a,	*fifth*	**décimo -a,**	*tenth*

The ordinal numbers are rarely used above *tenth*. When used as limiting adjectives, they precede the noun. When used to distinguish one thing from another, they follow the noun.

> **el tercer día**   *the third day*
> **la segunda parte**   *the second part*
> **lección décima**   *tenth lesson*
> *But:* **lección once**   *eleventh lesson (lesson eleven)*

Exercises

A. *Answer in Spanish.* 1. ¿Qué libro tiene don Juan? 2. ¿Cuánto tiempo hace que lo tiene? 3. ¿En qué año se lo trajo su padre? 4. ¿Qué le traía su padre siempre, cuando volvía de un viaje? 5. Según don Juan, ¿qué libro es el mejor del mundo? 6. ¿Cuántas veces lo ha leído? 7. ¿Piensa volver a leerlo? 8. ¿Por qué no lo ha leído Luis? 9. ¿Qué quiere saber Luis? 10. ¿En

qué año nació Miguel de Cervantes? 11. ¿En qué año murió?
12. ¿Qué autor inglés murió en el mismo año? 13. ¿Desde qué
punto de vista viven aún estos autores? 14. Según don Juan,
¿qué merece Cervantes? 15. ¿Qué clase de caballero nos presenta
Cervantes? 16. ¿Qué dice de este caballero Rubén Darío?
17. ¿En qué país nació Rubén Darío? 18. ¿De qué es ejemplo don
Quijote? 19. Según don Quijote mismo, ¿qué quiere hacer?
20. ¿Le parece a Vd. que hacen falta en el mundo tales locos?

B. *Translate.* 1. the first example; the first part 2. the third
point; the third person 3. good taste; a good view 4. a bad
effect; a bad habit 5. in some town; with some flowers 6. no
poet; no death 7. a great man; a large man

C. *Read aloud in Spanish and write.* 1. thirty-two gentlemen
2. forty-three poets 3. fifty-three points 4. sixty-five madmen
5. seventy-four works 6. eighty-six persons 7. ninety-nine
orders 8. one hundred laws 9. five hundred dresses 10. nine
hundred sixty-two companies 11. a thousand favors 12. three
million children

D. *Translate.* 1. Michael has been here for two days. 2. Another gentleman arrived an hour ago. 3. They need a horse,
don't they? 4. Have they enough money to buy it? 5. The truth
is that they haven't any money. 6. Please tell me what that
gentleman's name is. 7. He got up, closed the door, and sat down
again. 8. Those gentlemen do not have the same point of view.
9. Will you introduce me to your sister? 10. Don Quijote, although mad, was a good knight. 11. I have never known a man
of such virtue. 12. The first part of the *Quijote* came out (**salir**)
in the year 1605. 13. The second part came out one year before
the death of Cervantes. 14. Cervantes tried to understand the
eternal laws of nature. 15. A good poet deserves the thanks of
everybody. 16. According to the teacher, Rubén Darío was born
in 1867. 17. What does this word mean? 18. No man can tell
you that. 19. I myself can tell you. 20. We intend to return to
that place some day.

Vocabulary

NOUNS

el **bien,** good
el **caballero,** knight; gentleman
el **ejemplo,** example
la **falta,** lack, need
el **favor,** favor
el **gusto,** taste; pleasure
el **mal,** evil, harm
Miguel, Michael
el **poeta,** poet
el **punto,** point
la **virtud,** virtue

ADJECTIVES

eterno -a, eternal, everlasting
loco -a, mad, crazy; *noun,* madman
mismo -a, same; myself; yourself,
  himself, *etc.*

ninguno -a, no, not one; any; [1]
  pronoun, no one
tal, such; such a

VERBS

merecer, to merit, deserve
nacer, to be born
presentar, to present; to introduce
volver (ue), to turn; to return

ADVERBS

aun (*when emphatic, usually after
  the verb,* **aún**), still, yet; even
como, as, since
según, according to, as

OPTIONAL VOCABULARY

la semana, week

LOS DÍAS DE LA SEMANA

lunes,	Monday	**viernes,**	Friday
martes,	Tuesday	**sábado,**	Saturday
miércoles,	Wednesday	**domingo,**	Sunday
jueves,	Thursday		

el lunes	*on Monday*
los martes	*on Tuesdays*

Refrán

Del dicho al hecho hay gran trecho.
Saying and doing are two different things.

---

[1] When emphatic. The word *any,* unless emphatic, is not translated. **No tengo
dinero.** *I haven't any money.* **No tengo ningún dinero.** *I haven't any money.*

Lección Diecisiete

IDIOMS

con cuidado, carefully
de manera que, so, so that
llegar a ser, to get to be; to become
por lo menos, at least
subir a (un árbol), to climb (a tree)

Don Miguel estaba sentado junto al fuego. En el suelo delante de él había seis u ocho muchachos. Don Miguel les hablaba en español y ellos le escuchaban con cuidado para no perder nada de lo que decía el viejo español. Al fin, uno de los muchachos le preguntó:

— ¿De manera que ese Antonio era tío suyo, don Miguel?

— No, Juan, era antiguo amigo mío. Yo tenía un tío del mismo nombre, pero el mío vivía en Madrid. Ambos murieron hace muchos años. La verdad es que el tío Antonio no era tío de nadie, pero así le llamaba todo el mundo.

Pues, Antonio, a la edad de quince años, era el muchacho más vivo del pueblo, pero no quería estudiar. Huía de las clases para correr por los campos. Subía a los árboles más altos y siempre volvía a casa por la noche con los vestidos rotos. Era mucho más fuerte que los otros muchachos, y éstos se daban cuenta de que fácilmente podía romperles la cabeza. Así, Antonio era el que mandaba. Nos hablaba siempre de la guerra. Iba a ser un gran general. Iba a matar dos mil enemigos, por lo menos. Antonio, sin embargo, jamás llegó a ser general, y a la edad de cuarenta años no mataba más que el tiempo. Para el tío Antonio, el placer más grande del mundo era el de no hacer nada.

84. The Demonstrative Pronouns *el* (*la, los, las*) and *lo*

These demonstrative pronouns have the same form as the definite article. They are used in combination with **de** or **que** and in the formation of possessive pronouns (§ 86).

> **el de,** *that of, the one with* (*on, in*)
> **el que,** *that which, the one that, the one who*
> **lo que,** *what, that which*

Antonio era el que mandaba.	*Anthony was the one who commanded.*
Esta casa y la de mi padre.	*This house and my father's (that of my father).*
Ese hombre y el de los pies grandes.	*That man and the one with the big feet.*
Estos libros y los que están en el suelo.	*These books and the ones that are on the floor.*
¿Sabe Vd. lo que pasó?	*Do you know what (that which) happened?*

85. Possessive Adjectives That Follow the Noun

The possessive adjectives already studied (§ 24) are shortened forms of the following:

mío -a,	**míos -as,**	*my*
tuyo -a,	**tuyos -as,**	*your* (fam.)
suyo -a,	**suyos -as,**	*his, her, its, your*
nuestro -a,	**nuestros -as,**	*our*
vuestro -a,	**vuestros -as,**	*your* (fam.)
suyo -a,	**suyos -as,**	*their*

The above forms are used:
(a) in direct address

> Querido amigo mío. *My dear friend.*

(b) for English *of mine, of yours*, etc.

> Un tío suyo. *An uncle of yours.*

(c) after the verb **ser**

> No son míos. *They are not mine.*

86. Possessive Pronouns

The possessive pronouns are formed by placing the demonstrative **el** (**la, los, las**) before the possessive adjective. They agree with the thing possessed. **el mío, la mía,** *mine;* **el suyo, la suya,** *his, hers, yours, theirs,* etc.

Since **suyo** has several meanings, ambiguity is avoided when necessary by using the demonstrative **el** (**la,** etc.), followed by **de Vd., de él,** etc. After **ser,** the demonstrative is usually omitted.

Estas flores son más hermosas que las mías.	*These flowers are more beautiful than mine.*
¿Dónde están mis libros y los de Ana? Los suyos están en la mesa; los de ella están en el suelo.	*Where are my books and Anna's? Yours are on the table; hers are on the floor.*
Estas flores son de Vd.	*These flowers are yours.*

87. Negative Pronouns and Adverbs

Keep in mind that **no** is required before the verb when a negative pronoun or adverb follows it.

PRONOUNS	ADVERBS
nada, *nothing, anything*	**nunca,** *never, ever*
nadie, *no one, nobody, anybody*	**jamás,** *never, ever*
ninguno, *none, no one* (of them), *any* (of them)	

No halló nada.	*He found nothing* or *He didn't find anything.*
No lo sabe nadie or Nadie lo sabe.	*No one knows it.*
No veo a nadie.[1]	*I don't see anyone.*
Escribí a todos, pero ninguno ha venido.	*I wrote to all, but none* (of them) *has come.*
No mató a ninguno.[1]	*He didn't kill any* (of them).
No le veo nunca.	*I never see him.*
Jamás llegó a ser general.	*He never got to be a general.*

In an interrogative sentence, *ever* is **jamás** or **alguna vez.**

¿Le ha visto Vd. jamás?	*Have you ever seen him?*
¿Han vivido alguna vez en Méjico?	*Have they ever lived in Mexico?*

88. Present and Preterit Indicative of *huir*, *to flee* (See § 132, No. 11.)

PRESENT		PRETERIT	
huyo	huimos	huí	huimos
huyes	huís	huiste	huisteis
huye	huyen	huyó	huyeron

Exercises

A. *Answer in Spanish.* 1. ¿Dónde estaba sentado don Miguel?
2. ¿Dónde estaban los muchachos? 3. ¿Cuántos muchachos
había? 4. ¿Por qué escuchaban con cuidado? 5. ¿Qué preguntó uno de los niños? 6. ¿Cómo se llamaban los dos tíos?
7. ¿Dónde vivía el de don Miguel? 8. ¿Cuándo murieron estos
tíos? 9. ¿Cómo era Antonio a la edad de quince años? 10. Le
gustaban las clases? 11. ¿Qué hacía todos los días? 12. Al volver
a casa por la noche, ¿cómo tenía los vestidos? 13. Entre los
muchachos del pueblo, ¿quién era el que mandaba? 14. ¿De qué
se daban cuenta los demás? 15. ¿De qué hablaba siempre An-

---

[1] When **nadie** or **ninguno** (pronoun) is used as direct object, the "personal" **a** is
required.

tonio? 16. Según él mismo, ¿qué iba a ser? 17. ¿Qué iba a hacer?
18. ¿Llegó a ser general? 19. A la edad de cuarenta años, ¿qué
mataba el tío Antonio? 20. ¿Qué era el placer más grande del
mundo para él?

B. *Answer each question with a complete sentence, including the
word given in parentheses.* 1. ¿Mató al hombre? (nadie) 2. ¿Qué
ha roto Vd.? (nada) 3. ¿De quién huye Vd.? (nadie) 4. ¿Lo ha
visto Vd. alguna vez? (jamás) 5. ¿Habían salido todos los niños?
(ninguno) 6. ¿Corrían por los campos los dos muchachos?
(ambos) 7. ¿No le han dicho a Vd. nada? (algo) 8. ¿No viene
nadie? (alguien)

C. *Read aloud, translating the italicized words.* 1. Tengo *my*
libros y *yours*. 2. Estas cosas son *mine;* aquéllas son *theirs*.
3. María es antigua amiga *of mine*. 4. ¿Mataron *your* caballos o
Michael's? 5. ¿Rompió el niño *our* cartas o *those* que estaban en
the floor? 6. *¿Do you ever run* por los campos? 7. Pepe *never
runs*. 8. No entendió *what* Vd. dijo. 9. Yo no dije *anything*.
10. *Nobody* dijo *anything*. 11. Antonio *never got to be* maestro.
12. Había cuatro personas, pero *none* sabía *my name* ni *that of*
mi amigo.

D. *Translate.* 1. It was a cold night. 2. John and some friends
of his were sitting by the fire. 3. There were seven or eight, at
least. 4. John was telling them something. 5. Please tell me
what he was saying. 6. Someone had killed a man. 7. They
found him in the street with his head broken. 8. The one who
killed him fled. 9. Nobody saw him, although there were people
in the street. 10. How long ago did this happen? 11. Four days
ago, but listen carefully. 12. I'm going to tell you what happened
last night. 13. Two men were walking along (**por**) the street.
14. Finally they realized that there was someone behind them.
15. On turning their heads,[1] they saw a man with his clothes

---

[1] **la cabeza.** When referring to a single part of the body or article of clothing possessed by each one of a group, Spanish generally uses the singular. How many
heads does each man turn?

torn. 16. So Anthony, the madman, was the one who killed him?
17. Yes. He thought the old man was an enemy of his. 18. After
killing him, Anthony climbed a tall tree. 19. The poor old man
wasn't anybody's enemy. 20. His greatest pleasure was that of
doing nothing. 21. At the age of twelve he was a lively boy.
22. He would (used to) run from here to the river in half an hour.
23. He was stronger and livelier than the rest. 24. In spite of
that, he never got to be the one who commanded.

Vocabulary

NOUNS

Antonio, Anthony
el cuidado, care
la edad, age
el enemigo, enemy
el fuego, fire
la manera, manner, way
el nombre, name
el placer, pleasure
el suelo, floor, ground

PRONOUNS

alguien, someone, somebody
ambos, both; *adj.*, both
nadie, no one, nobody, anybody

ADJECTIVES

antiguo -a, old
fuerte, strong
roto -a,[1] broken, torn
vivo -a, alive, lively; bright

VERBS

correr, to run
escuchar, to listen (to)
huir, to flee
matar, to kill
romper, to break, tear

ADVERBS

así, so, thus
jamás, never, ever

CONJUNCTION

u, or (*before a word beginning with*
o or **ho**)

OPTIONAL VOCABULARY

pasado mañana, day after tomorrow
la semana pasada, last week
la semana que viene, next week

Refrán

Condiciones rompen leyes.
Circumstances alter cases.

---

[1] Irregular past participle of **romper,** *to break, tear.*

Lección Dieciocho

IDIOMS

de nada, you are welcome; don't mention it
dejar de (+ *inf.*), to stop; to fail; **no deje Vd. de
 hacerlo,** do not fail to do it
en cambio, on the other hand
en voz alta, in a loud voice
¡Está bien! Right!

—Mañana les contaré a Vds. un cuento en español. Estoy
seguro de que el cuento les gustará, por ser [1] una historia verdadera. Procuraré hablar en voz alta y clara. No dejen Vds. de
aprender bien las palabras que se hallan en este papel. Así
podrán comprender el cuento. En cambio, si no aprenden las
palabras, no comprenderán nada. Les advierto a Vds. que no
podrán gozar del cuento sin saber todas las palabras. Deben
aprenderse hoy. No las dejen Vds. para mañana.

—No olvide Vd., don Juan, lo que nos dijo ayer.

—Pues, ¿qué les dije ayer, Miguel?

—Nos dijo que hoy hablaríamos del cuerpo humano.

—Tiene Vd. razón, y ahora dígame algunas partes del cuerpo.

—La cabeza, el pecho, los brazos, las manos, y los pies son las
partes principales del cuerpo humano. La frente, los ojos, y la
boca son partes de la cara. Dentro del pecho se halla el corazón.

---

[1] **por ser = porque es.**

— ¡Está bien! ¿Para qué sirve [1] el corazón, Miguel?

— El corazón hace correr la sangre a todas partes del cuerpo.
La sangre sube a la cabeza y baja a los pies.

— Muy bien dicho.

— ¿Me hará Vd. el favor de decirme qué hora es, don Juan?

— Serán las cuatro, Miguel. Hemos hablado más de dos horas,
y basta por hoy. Vendrán Vds. mañana a la misma hora, ¿verdad?

— Sí, señor, y mil gracias.

— De nada. Me gustaría hablar más, pero no tengo tiempo.

89. The Future Indicative

The future is formed by adding to the infinitive the endings of
the present tense of **haber: é, ás, á, emos, éis, án.** All forms, except the first plural, have the written accent.

hablar	comer	vivir
hablaré	comeré	viviré
hablarás	comerás	vivirás
hablará	comerá	vivirá
hablaremos	comeremos	viviremos
hablaréis	comeréis	viviréis
hablarán	comerán	vivirán

90. The Conditional

The endings of the conditional, added to the infinitive, are
those of the imperfect of **haber: ía, ías, ía, íamos, íais, ían.**

hablar	comer	vivir
hablaría	comería	viviría
hablarías	comerías	vivirías
hablaría	comería	viviría
hablaríamos	comeríamos	viviríamos
hablaríais	comeríais	viviríais
hablarían	comerían	vivirían

---

[1] ¿Para qué sirve . . . *What is the function of* . . . (lit., *For what serves* . . .).

91. Irregular Stems in the Future and Conditional

All verbs have regular endings in the future and conditional, but the following have irregular stems.

INFINITIVE	FUTURE	CONDITIONAL
haber	habré, etc.	habría, etc.
poder	podré	podría
querer	querré	querría
saber	sabré	sabría
poner	pondré	pondría
tener	tendré	tendría
venir	vendré	vendría
salir	saldré	saldría
valer	valdré	valdría
decir	diré	diría
hacer	haré	haría

92. Uses of the Future and Conditional

1. The future is usually translated as in English: *I shall, you will,* etc. It also expresses probability or conjecture with reference to the present.

Mañana les contaré a Vds. un cuento.	*Tomorrow I shall tell you a story.*
Pepe no podrá comprenderlo.	*Joe will not be able to understand it.*
¿Qué hora es? Serán las cuatro.	*What time is it? It must be (probably is) four o'clock.*
¿Quién será?	*Who can it be?*
Será mi padre.	*It must be (probably is) my father.*

2. The conditional is usually translated *would (should).* It also expresses probability or conjecture with reference to past time.

Dijo que vendría.	*He said that he would come.*
Me gustaría hacerlo.	*I should like to do it.*
¿Qué hora era? Sería la una.	*What time was it? It must have been one o'clock.*

3. Remember that *will*, in the sense of *be willing to*, and *would not*, in the sense of *was not willing (refused) to*, require **querer** Remember also that *should* in the sense of *ought to* is **deber.**

No quiere hacerlo.	*He will not do it.*
No quiso hacerlo.	*He would not do it.*
No debe decir eso.	*He shouldn't say that.*

93. The Reflexive to Express Passive Voice

The reflexive verb is frequently used in Spanish to express passive voice, especially when the subject is a thing. Usually the passive subject follows the verb.

Dentro del pecho se halla el corazón.	*The heart is found in the breast.*
En Méjico se habla español.	*Spanish is spoken in Mexico.*
Las palabras deben aprenderse hoy.	*The words should be learned today.*

94. The Interrogative *¿cuál?*

What is (are), followed by a noun, is *¿***Cuál es** (*¿***Cuáles son**), except when a definition is called for.

¿Cuáles son las partes principales del cuerpo?	*What are the principal parts of the body?*
But: ¿Qué es agua?	*What is water?*

Exercises

A. *Answer in Spanish.* 1. ¿Qué contará don Juan mañana? 2. ¿De qué está seguro don Juan? 3. ¿Qué clase de cuento es? 4. ¿De qué manera procurará hablar don Juan? 5. ¿Qué han de hacer los muchachos antes de oír el cuento? 6. ¿Podrán comprender la historia? 7. ¿Qué les advierte don Juan? 8. ¿Cuándo deben aprenderse las palabras? 9. Según Miguel, ¿qué dijo ayer don Juan? 10. ¿Cuáles son las partes principales del cuerpo humano? 11. ¿Para qué sirve la lengua? 12. ¿Para qué sirve el corazón?

B. *Read aloud, translating the italicized words.* 1. *I warned you* que no vendría. 2. *Lower* Vd. la cabeza. 3. *They are counting* las palabras. 4. *It is enough*, y no diga Vd. más. 5. Al entrar yo, *they stopped* hablar. 6. *Leave him* en paz. 7. *They have left* las cosas en la mesa. 8. *I was trying* no olvidarlo. 9. *He served* al rey. 10. *Do not tell me* (**contar**) tales cosas.

C. *Write a synopsis* (*present, imperfect, preterit, future, and conditional*) *of each verb.* 1. bajar (*1st sing.*) 2. querer (*3d sing.*) 3. saber (*3d pl.*) 4. poner (*1st pl.*) 5. tener (*1st sing.*) 6. salir (*3d sing.*) 7. decir (*1st sing.*) 8. hacer (*3d pl.*)

D. *Translate.* 1. Someone is at the door. 2. Who can it be? 3. It must be Charles. 4. He said that he would come at eight. 5. Here he comes with his arms full of books. 6. He will tell you a good story. 7. Please read this one to us, Charles. 8. It is a true story, isn't it? 9. As for that, I think not. 10. Nevertheless, I think you will like it. 11. It treats of the causes and of the effects of war. 12. Much blood is lost. 13. Many heads are broken. 14. On the other hand, you will find some beautiful pictures in the book. 15. Of course, the main point is found at the end of the story. 16. Listen carefully, while I read a few words. 17. Charles speaks in a loud, clear voice. 18. Mary, are you sure that you understand what he says? 19. I understand every word that comes (**salir**) from his mouth. 20. The forehead is a part of the face. 21. Please write the words that mean *breast* and *heart*. 22. Many thanks. Don't mention it.

Vocabulary

NOUNS

el **brazo,** arm
la **boca,** mouth
el **cambio,** change
la **cara,** face
el **corazón,** heart
el **cuento,** story
el **cuerpo,** body
la **frente,** forehead
el **pecho,** breast, chest

la **sangre,** blood
la **voz,** voice

ADJECTIVES

claro -a, clear
humano -a, human
principal, principal, main
seguro -a, sure
verdadero -a, true, real

VERBS

advertir (ie), to warn
bajar, to go down; to lower
bastar, to be enough
contar (ue), to count; to tell, relate
dejar, to leave
olvidar, to forget
procurar, to try
servir (i), to serve

OPTIONAL VOCABULARY

el dedo, finger, toe
el diente, tooth
el labio, lip; labio superior (inferior), upper (lower) lip
la nariz, nose
la oreja, ear
el pelo, hair
la pierna, leg
el rostro, face

INTERROGATIVE

¿cuál? (*pl.*, ¿cuáles?), what? which?

Refrán

En boca cerrada no entran moscas.
A closed mouth catches no flies.

Lección Diecinueve

IDIOMS

de pronto, suddenly
dirigirse a, to make one's way toward
en seguida, at once, immediately
la mar de cosas, a (the) mass of things
libro de memorias, memorandum book
quiere a (María), he loves (Mary)
volverse loco, to become (go) crazy

— Antonio, vaya Vd. a mi cuarto, saque el librito de memorias y búsqueme el número de la casa del señor Contreras. El librito está en la mesita.

— En seguida. Ese librito es de color blanco, ¿verdad?

— No, Antonio. No es blanco sino negro, tan negro como los ojos de María.

— Pues entonces será negrísimo. Vd. quiere mucho a María, ¿verdad, señorito?

— Muchísimo. La quiero con toda mi alma, con mis cinco sentidos, con . . .

— ¡Basta, señorito! Con tanto amor va Vd. a volverse loco.

— Pues, dígame ¿ha conocido Vd. jamás mujer más bella que María?

— Ni más rica. Se dice que es riquísima.

— ¡Calle Vd.! No me caso con ella porque tiene dinero. Ya tengo bastante yo mismo.

Antonio va al cuarto de Carlos y se pone a buscar el librito
de memorias entre la mar de cosas que se hallan en la mesita.
Cuando al fin lo encuentra, el suelo queda cubierto de cartas y
papeles. De pronto, se oye la voz de Carlos.

— ¡Hombre! ¿Qué hace Vd. ahí? Recoja esas cartas. Son de
mi María y valen más que el oro. Mire Vd. esa letra; bellísima,
¿no? Ponga las cartas en la mesita y sígame. Vamos a casa del
señor Contreras.

Antonio recoge las cartas y los papeles. Los pone sobre la mesita.
Después sale del cuarto y se dirige al lugar donde le espera Carlos.

95. Orthographic-Changing Verbs [1]

In order to preserve the final consonant sound of the verb stem,
a change in spelling is often necessary. Review the following:
(**k,** as in *keep;* **g,** as in *go;* **th,** as in *thin;* **h,** as in *hawk*)

(k)	ca, co, cu, que, qui
(g)	ga, go, gu, gue, gui
(th)	za, zo, zu, ce, ci
(h)	ja, jo, ju, ge, gi

1. Verbs in **-car, -gar, -zar**

	PRETERIT	COMMAND FORM
sacar:	saqué, sacaste, etc.	saque
llegar:	llegué, llegaste, etc.	llegue
empezar:	empecé, empezaste, etc.	empiece

2. Verbs in **-ger** and **-gir**

	PRESENT	COMMAND FORM
recoger:	recojo, recoges, etc.	recoja
dirigir:	dirijo, diriges, etc.	dirija

3. Verbs in **-guir**

	PRESENT	COMMAND FORM
seguir	sigo, sigues, etc.	siga

---

[1] See § 132.

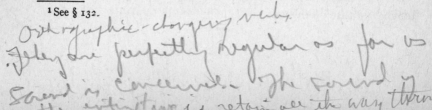

96. Comparisons of Equality

The correlatives used in comparisons of equality are: **tan . . . como,** *as . . . as* and **tanto -a (tantos -as) . . . como,** *as much (as many) . . . as.*

Es tan negro como los ojos de María.	*It is as black as Mary's eyes.*
Juan es tan pobre como Vd.	*John is as poor as you.*
Ana no tiene tanto dinero como María.	*Anna hasn't as much money as Mary.*
Esta palabra tiene tantas letras como aquélla.	*This word has as many letters as that one.*

97. The Absolute Superlative

The absolute superlative is formed by attaching to the adjective the ending **-ísimo -a.** It merely indicates a high degree of the quality expressed by the adjective.

Ojos negrísimos.	*Very black eyes.*
Muchísimo.	*Very much.*
Se dice que es riquísima.	*It is said that she is very rich.*
Tiene una letra bellísima.	*She has an exceedingly beautiful handwriting.*

98. The Conjunction *sino*

When the conjunction *but* introduces a positive statement in direct contrast with a preceding negative statement, it must be translated by **sino.**

El libro no es blanco, sino negro.	*The book is not white, but black.*
No me habló en francés, sino en español.	*He did not speak to me in French, but in Spanish.*

99. Diminutives

Spanish makes frequent use of diminutive endings to express small size or affectionate interest. The commonest are: **-ito, -cito,**

-ecito, and -illo. Drop the final vowel of a word before adding the suffix. *cabeza head   cabecita, little head*

hermano, *brother*	hermanito, *little brother*
Juan, *John*	Juanito, *Johnny*
mesa, *table*	mesita, *little table, stand*
libro, *book*	librito, *little book*
hombre, *man*	hombrecito, *little man*
joven, *young man*	jovencito, *young fellow*
viejo, *old man*	viejecito, *nice old man*
mujer, *woman*	mujercita, *little woman*
pueblo, *town*	pueblecito, *little town, village*
flor, *flower*	florecita, *little flower*

casa, house   casita little house

Exercises

A. *Answer in Spanish.* 1. ¿Dónde está el librito de memorias? 2. ¿Quién ha de sacarlo? 3. ¿Por qué quiere Carlos el librito? 4. ¿De qué color es el librito? 5. ¿Quién tiene los ojos muy negros? 6. ¿Quién quiere mucho a María? 7. ¿Cuántos sentidos tenemos? 8. Según Antonio, ¿quién va a volverse loco? 9. ¿Qué le pregunta Carlos a Antonio? 10. ¿Es pobre María? 11. ¿Cree Vd. que le gustaría a Antonio casarse con una muchacha rica? 12. ¿Cuántas cosas se hallan en la mesita? 13. Cuando al fin Antonio encuentra el librito, ¿cómo queda el suelo? 14. De pronto, ¿qué se oye en el cuarto? 15. Según Carlos, ¿cuánto valen las cartas? 16. ¿Qué clase de letra tiene María? 17. Antes de salir, ¿qué hace Antonio? 18. Al salir, ¿adónde se dirige?

B. *Translate.* 1. I got out my books. 2. They took out the horses. 3. I arrived at nine o'clock. 4. He arrived at twelve. 5. I began to read. 6. You began to talk. 7. I pick up the papers. 8. They pick up the books. 9. I direct him. 10. They go (make their way) toward the house. 11. I follow him. 12. Are you following me? 13. Look for the letter. 14. Arrive first. 15. Begin (*pl.*) at once. 16. Pick up those things. 17. Direct [1] Mr. Jones to

---

[1] Use the redundant construction.

my house. 18. Follow us. 19. Take him out. 20. He has gone crazy.

C. *Read aloud in Spanish.* 1. a hundred thousand souls 2. so many letters (*of the alphabet*) 3. so many numbers 4. as rich as a king 5. very pretty colors 6. exceedingly high mountains 7. a few little things 8. the child's little head 9. my little brother 10. so many little towns 11. that little man 12. these little flowers

D. *Translate.* 1. Uncle Frank is sitting near the window. 2. He is looking at the people in the street. 3. Suddenly a voice is heard. 4. On turning his head, Uncle Frank sees Johnny. 5. "Please tell me a story," says Johnny. 6. "Gladly " says the nice old man. 7. Many years ago there was a little woman who lived in a little house near the sea. 8. She was not rich, but poor. 9. She had a son who loved her very much. 10. "Love is worth more than gold," she often said to him. 11. One day the son was going along the road. 12. Suddenly he realized that someone was calling him. 13. Then he saw a white object on the ground. 14. Farther on there was a black horse. 15. It was an exceedingly beautiful animal. 16. The boy made his way toward the place. 17. He soon realized that the object was a girl dressed in (**de**) white. 18. The horse had thrown her to the ground. 19. Her eyes were closed. 20. The young man thought that she was dead. 21. He had never seen a face so white. 22. Nevertheless, the color soon began to return to her face. 23. She opened her eyes and spoke to him. 24. Did he marry her later, Uncle Frank? 25. Yes, Johnny, he married her thirty-nine years ago. 26. What a memory! I mean forty-one years ago.

Vocabulary

NOUNS

el alma *f.*, soul
el amor, love
el color, color

la letra, letter (*of the alphabet*); handwriting
la mar, sea [1]

---

[1] mar is either masculine or feminine. When used figuratively to mean a large quantity, it is feminine. Its use as a feminine noun predominates.

NOUNS

la memoria, memory; memorandum
la mujer, woman
el número, number
el oro, gold
la seguida (*see Idioms*)
el sentido, sense
el señorito, young gentleman; Mr. (*used by servants*)

ADJECTIVES

bello -a, beautiful
blanco -a, white
negro -a, black
tanto -a, so much, as much; *pl.*, so many, as many

VERBS

callar, to be silent; to keep quiet
casarse (con), to marry, get married
dirigir, to direct
mirar, to look (at)

recoger, to pick up
sacar, to take out; to get out
seguir (i), to follow; to continue

ADVERBS

pronto, quickly, soon
tan, so, as

CONJUNCTION

sino, but

OPTIONAL VOCABULARY

el hambre *f.*, hunger; **tiene mucha hambre,** he is very hungry
el miedo, fear; **tiene miedo,** he is afraid
el pelo, hair; **tiene el pelo negro,** he has black hair
la prisa, haste, hurry; **tiene prisa,** he is in a hurry
la sed, thirst; **tiene sed,** he is thirsty

Refrán

No es oro todo lo que reluce.
All is not gold that glitters.

Lección Veinte

IDIOMS

a la derecha, to (at, on) the right
a propósito, by the way
atreverse a, to dare
bien considerado, on second thought
esta noche, tonight
por primera vez, for the first time
tal vez, perhaps

— ¿Sabe Vd. que la compañía de don José Valdés acaba de llegar al Teatro Real? Se dice que Mendoza forma parte de la compañía y que don José le paga dos mil pesos al mes.

— Pues, que don José tenga mejor suerte esta vez. Tendrá que ganar mucho para pagar a Mendoza. Vd. le ha oído cantar, ¿verdad?

— Sí, varias veces, pero deseo que Miguel le oiga.

— Muy bien, que venga con nosotros. Estoy seguro de [1] que le gustará la voz de Mendoza. ¿Qué hora es?

— Serán las ocho. Vámonos.

— Un momento. Que vaya el criado a traer aquí a Miguel. ¡Antonio! (*Un instante después el criado aparece con los brazos*

---

[1] If a noun or adjective requires a preposition to connect it with its complement (**Estoy seguro** *de* **esto**, *I am sure of this*), the preposition is retained when the complement is a noun clause introduced by **que**.

llenos de libros.) Deje Vd. esos libros aquí en la mesa y vaya a casa de Miguel. Dígale que venga pronto. Vamos al Teatro Real y queremos que nos acompañe.

(*En el teatro*)

— ¿Quién va a cantar esta noche, Miguel? No será Mendoza porque está malo. Al salir del teatro anoche cayó al suelo. Tuvieron que llevarle a casa. No será cosa grave, sin embargo. Había trabajado mucho y estaba cansado. ¿Quién va a cantar en su lugar?

— No tengo la menor idea. Es un secreto. Se lo pregunté al caballero que está sentado detrás de mí. Contestó que no lo sabía.

— A la derecha de Vd. está la señora de Valdés. ¿Se atreve Vd. a preguntárselo?

— No, señor, no me atrevo. No tengo el gusto de conocerla.

— Mire Vd. Aquí viene la familia de Contreras. A propósito, el señor Contreras canta muy bien. Ha cantado en los mejores teatros de su tierra. Dicen que canta mejor que Mendoza.

— Será el que canta esta noche, ¿no?

— Tal vez. Pero, bien considerado, me parece que no. Según lo que me dijo Luis, el que presentan esta noche aparece ante el público por primera vez.

— Pues, que cante en seguida. Serán cerca de las nueve.

100. The Present Subjunctive

The stem of the present subjunctive of all regular and of most irregular verbs is that of the first person singular present indicative.[1] For -ar verbs, present subjunctive endings are: e, es, e, emos, éis, en; for -er and -ir verbs: a, as, a, amos, áis, an.

---

[1] Since the command form (§ 76) is present subjunctive, this stem has already been given.

hablar	comer	vivir
hable	coma	viva
hables	comas	vivas
hable	coma	viva
hablemos	comamos	vivamos
habléis	comáis	viváis
hablen	coman	vivan

101. Present Subjunctive of *dar, estar, ir, saber,* and *ser*

The present subjunctive of these verbs must be learned separately since they do not follow the above rule.

dar	estar	ir	saber	ser
dé	esté	vaya	sepa	sea
des	estés	vayas	sepas	seas
dé	esté	vaya	sepa	sea
demos	estemos	vayamos	sepamos	seamos
deis	estéis	vayáis	sepáis	seáis
den	estén	vayan	sepan	sean

102. Present Subjunctive of Radical-Changing Verbs

The present subjunctive of -ar and -er radical-changing verbs is regular: (encontrar) encuentre, etc., (entender) entienda, etc. -ir verbs change e to i and o to u in the first and second persons plural. See § 130.

sentir	morir	pedir
sienta	muera	pida
sientas	mueras	pidas
sienta	muera	pida
sintamos	muramos	pidamos
sintáis	muráis	pidáis
sientan	mueran	pidan

103. The Subjunctive in Indirect Commands

The subjunctive is used in direct commands (the command form). It is also used in indirect commands. When so used, it is preceded by **que**, except in the first person plural. The construction with **que** may also express a wish or hope.

Que venga Miguel	*Let Michael come.*
Que vaya el criado.	*Let (have) the servant go.*
Que canten en seguida.	*Let them sing at once.*
Cantemos [1] todos.	*Let's all sing.*
Vámonos. [2]	*Let's go.*
Que tenga mejor suerte.	*May he have better luck.*

104. The Subjunctive in Noun Clauses

A noun clause is a clause used as the subject or object of a verb. The principal use of the subjunctive is in dependent clauses, introduced by the conjunctive **que**. It is required in dependent noun clauses after verbs expressing *will* or *desire;* that is, when one person (the subject of the main verb) expresses his will or desire that another (the subject of the dependent verb) do or not do the thing indicated.

Dígale que venga.	*Tell him to come.*
Deseo que Vd. le oiga.	*I want you to hear him.*
Quieren que lo sepamos.	*They want us to know it.*
Le escribo que esté aquí a las dos.	*I am writing him to be here at two o'clock.*

105. Position of Dependent Infinitive after Verbs of Sense Perception (*ver, oír,* etc.)

---

[1] As an affirmative command in the first person plural, **vamos a** . . . is frequently used. **Vamos a cantar.** *Let's sing.*

[2] In the expression *Let's go,* **vamos** is used instead of **vayamos.** If the verb is reflexive, the final **-s** is dropped before the reflexive pronoun **nos** is added.

A dependent infinitive is usually placed immediately after the main verb, when the latter is a verb of sense perception.

Oyeron cantar a Mendoza.	*They heard Mendoza sing.*
Vi correr al niño.	*I saw the child run.*

106. caer, *to fall*

PRESENT		PRETERIT [1]	
caigo	caemos	caí	caímos
caes	caéis	caíste	caísteis
cae	caen	cayó	cayeron

Exercises

A. *Answer in Spanish.* 1. ¿Qué compañía acaba de llegar al Teatro Real? 2. ¿Quién forma parte de la compañía? 3. ¿Cuánto va a ganar Mendoza? 4. Antes de venir al Teatro Real, ¿qué suerte ha tenido don José? 5. ¿Por qué tendrá que ganar mucho dinero don José? 6. ¿Le gustaría a Vd. oír cantar a Mendoza? 7. ¿Cómo se llama el criado? 8. Al entrar éste, ¿qué le dice el joven? 9. ¿Por qué no cantará Mendoza esta noche? 10. ¿Qué le pasó anoche? 11. ¿Saben los muchachos quién va a cantar en lugar de Mendoza? 12. ¿A quién se lo pregunta uno de ellos? 13. ¿Qué contesta el caballero? 14. ¿Dónde está sentada la señora de Valdés? 15. ¿Qué no se atreve a hacer el joven? 16. ¿Dónde ha cantado el señor Contreras? 17. ¿Cómo sabe el joven que Contreras no va a cantar esta noche? 18. ¿Ha cantado Vd. alguna vez ante el público?

B. *Translate.* 1. Eat the meat. 2. Let Joe eat it. 3. Let us consider it a moment. 4. Let them answer at once. 5. Have the servant come in. 6. Let's go, my friends. 7. Let's pay for it now.

---

[1] The verbs **caer, creer, leer,** and **oír** change the **i** of the preterit endings **-ió** and **-ieron** to **y**. Note also that the **i** of the first person plural and of the second person, singular and plural, must have a written accent. See § 132, No. 9.

8. I wish to form a company.[1] 9. I wish you to form it. 10. Write him not to buy the house. 11. He wants me to sing tonight. 12. Tell them to bring the money. 13. May you live many years! 14. May you (*pl.*) enjoy good health!

C. *Translate.* 1. What fell a moment ago, Anthony? 2. I haven't the least idea, sir. 3. An instant afterward, I saw Johnny run. 4. By the way, I have something for him. 5. It is in my room, behind the door to the right. 6. I don't want Johnny to see it yet. 7. Well, he wouldn't dare to enter your room. 8. Perhaps, but get it out. 9. It would be better to put it in another place. 10. Do you wish me to put it in my room? 11. No, Anthony, on second thought I ought to show it to him. 12. Did you ask Contreras whether he is to sing tonight? 13. Yes, sir, but he didn't answer me. 14. Are you sure that (**de que**) he heard you? 15. The maid tells me that he is ill. 16. May it not be a serious matter (**cosa**)! 17. It is a secret, but I know that Joseph is to sing in his place. 18. Do you mean the one who has just formed the company? 19. Yes, he will sing in the Royal Theater. 20. He will appear before the public tonight for the first time. 21. Two men from his (native) country are to appear with him. 22. May he not regret it later! 23. By the way, his mother has never heard him sing. 24. May she not die before hearing him!

Vocabulary

NOUNS

el criado, servant; la criada, servant girl, maid
la idea, idea
el instante, instant
José, Joseph
el momento, moment

el propósito, purpose
el público, public
el secreto, secret
la suerte, luck
la tierra, earth, land; (native) country

---

[1] No dependent clause, since the subject of the main verb is also the subject of the dependent infinitive.

ADJECTIVES

derecho -a, right
grave, grave, serious
real, royal; real

VERBS

aparecer, to appear
atreverse (a), to dare
caer, to fall
cantar, to sing
considerar, to consider
contestar, to answer
desear, to desire

formar, to form
pagar, to pay; to pay for

PREPOSITION

ante, before (*place*)

OPTIONAL VOCABULARY

la contestación, answer
la respuesta, answer
izquierdo -a, left; **a la iz-
quierda,** to (at, on) the left
la pregunta, question; **hacer una
pregunta,** to ask a question

Refrán

Quien no se atreve no pasa la mar.
Nothing ventured, nothing won (Faint heart ne'er won fair lady).

Repaso

A. *Translate.* 1. thirty-seven gentlemen. 2. forty-nine points 3. fifty-three names 4. sixty-five servants 5. seventy-four months 6. eighty-one faces 7. ninety-two arms 8. a hundred hearts 9. three hundred stories 10. five hundred souls 11. nine hundred bodies 12. a thousand colors 13. a hundred thousand fires 14. a million enemies 15. ten million pesos 16. in 1492

B. *Translate.* 1. They were born in 1807. 2. Both died at the age of fifty-one. 3. The first man married in 1831, the second, one year later. 4. He fled from Spain in the year 1840. 5. I climbed the mountain today for the first time. 6. This boy is the one who brought you the flowers. 7. A thousand thanks. Don't mention it. 8. Have you ever seen more beautiful flowers? 9. Never. I like especially those that you left on the table. 10. I did not leave them on the table, but on the floor. 11. They need water, don't they? 12. Yes, that is what they need. 13. Look at them. They don't seem as beautiful this morning. 14. Listen. Someone is coming. 15. Perhaps, but I don't hear anybody. 16. It is probably one of the maids. 17. As a matter of fact, I saw them go out and none has returned.

C. *Translate.* 1. Michael has been counting his money for half an hour. 2. For four months he has been earning more than a hundred dollars a month. 3. For some time he and some friends of his have desired to form a company. 4. They consider themselves exceedingly rich. 5. How long had Michael been serving you before coming here? 6. He did not serve me, but my uncle. 7. What is the name of the company? 8. I haven't the least idea.

D. *Translate.* 1. Will you do the work tomorrow? 2. I think

I shall be able to do it. 3. Are you sure that you will know how to do it? 4. How much will it be worth? 5. You will have to ask [1] Mr. Pérez. 6. Yes, he probably knows. 7. He said he would come at four o'clock. 8. He will wish to speak to you at once. 9. Will they put my name and yours on the paper? 10. They said they would put them on both papers. 11. Will they tell me where to find Mr. Pérez? 12. I am sure that they will tell you.[1]

E. *Translate the italicized words, then translate the completed sentence into English.* 1. *¿Do you mean* que Miguel *is a good example* para los otros? 2. *That's it,* y *some* día será *a great* hombre. 3. *Please* presentarme a su amigo. 4. *I would do it gladly,* pero he olvidado el número de su casa. 5. Tengo una memoria *so bad* que algunas veces olvido *mine.* 6. *By the way,* ¿le veré a Vd. esta noche? 7. *Perhaps,* pero tengo un fuerte dolor *in my right eye.* 8. ¿Qué le pasó, *my son?* 9. *I was running* por la calle cuarenta y nueve. 10. *Continue,* ¿qué le pasó? 11. *Something fell* sobre mi cabeza. 12. ¿Por qué *didn't you return at once* a casa? 13. *I didn't dare* volver con la frente llena de sangre. 14. *I did not wish* aparecer así ante mi madre. 15. *Suddenly* perdí los sentidos. 16. Según Luis, su madre de Vd. *loves you very much.* 17. Naturalmente, *mothers* siempre *love their* hijos.

F. *Translate the italicized words.* 1. *I got out* pluma y papel. 2. *I began* a escribir. 3. Luis, *get out yours.* 4. *I paid for* mi casa y *theirs.* 5. *Pick up* estas cosas y *those.* 6. *Tell them to follow* este camino. 7. Mientras ella canta, *let him keep quiet.* 8. *Let's try* comprenderle. 9. Escríbales *not to come* hoy. 10. Quiero *you to answer me* mañana.

---

[1] See note 1, p. 48.

Lección Veintiuna

IDIOMS

coge del brazo a (su amigo), he seizes (his friend) by the arm
cumplir (diez) **años**, to reach one's (tenth) birthday
hace (mucho) **calor**, it is (very) warm
hay sol, the sun is shining
por el camino, along the road
puesto que, since (*causal*)

El tío Paco y el tío Pepe andan por el camino que conduce al río Guadalquivir.[1] Hay sol y hace muchísimo calor. El tío Paco tiene sesenta años y su amigo acaba de cumplir sesenta y seis. Ambos viejecitos gozan de buena salud, pero ya no andan con paso rápido.

Hace más de treinta años que el tío Paco sirve a don Carlos, un señor riquísimo que tiene tierras y casas dentro y fuera de la ciudad de Córdoba. En una de estas casas vive el tío Paco con su esposa, María. No gana mucho. Sin embargo, tiene dinero, puesto que ha procurado guardar siete u ocho duros cada mes durante los treinta años.

El tío Pepe tiene su propia casa. Además, tiene unas tierras cerca del río Guadalquivir. Ya no tiene fuerzas para trabajarlas todas y quiere que Paco compre parte de ellas. Por eso le lleva al río.

---

[1] The Guadalquivir is the principal river of Andalusia (southern Spain). On its shores are located two of Spain's most important cities, Córdoba and Sevilla. *Guadalquivir* is an Arabic word meaning *río grande*.

De pronto el tío Paco se detiene, coge del brazo a su amigo y le dice: — Siento que no hayamos comenzado este viaje antes de levantarse el sol. ¡Qué calor! Si no me ayuda Dios, me parece que no llego nunca al río. Tengo los pies como dos piedras. Apenas puedo moverlos.

— ¡Pues entonces que Dios le ayude! Quiero que vea Vd. esas tierras y que las compre.

— Pero hombre, no es preciso que las vea hoy. Podría Vd. mostrármelas mañana. Además, Vd. me pide mil quinientos duros. Mucho dinero me parece por unas tierras que son más duras que una piedra. Dice mi amo que no producen nada.

— ¡Naturalmente! ¿Y por qué lo dice? Teme que Vd. las compre. Teme que Vd. deje de servirle. Además, quiere que Vd. compre las suyas.

— Es posible que tenga Vd. razón, Pepe. También es posible que Vd. se dé cuenta de [1] que esas tierras no valen mil quinientos duros y que me las ofrezca por menos. ¡Vámonos!

107. The Present Perfect Subjunctive

The present perfect subjunctive is formed with the present subjunctive of **haber** and the past participle.

haya hablado	hayamos hablado
hayas hablado	hayáis hablado
haya hablado	hayan hablado

108. Subjunctive in Noun Clauses (*continued*)

We have seen that the subjunctive is used in dependent noun clauses after verbs expressing *will* or *desire* (wish, command, request). The subjunctive is also used in such clauses (a) after verbs expressing *emotion* (hope, fear, regret, etc.); (b) after certain *impersonal expressions* implying necessity, opinion, etc.: **es preciso**

---

[1] See note 1, p. 113.

(necesario) que, es imposible que, importa que, etc.; and (c) after expressions that indicate *uncertainty* in the mind of the speaker: dudo que, no creo que, es posible que, etc.

(a) Espero que me las ofrezca a mí.	*I hope he will offer them to me.*
Teme que el tío Paco deje de servirle.	*He fears that Uncle Frank may stop serving him.*
Siento que Vd. no haya visto las tierras.	*I regret that you have not seen the lands.*
(b) Es necesario que Vd. vaya a verlas.	*It is necessary that you go to see them.*
No es preciso que las vea hoy.	*It isn't necessary that I see them today.*
No importa que sean duras.	*It doesn't matter that they are hard.*
(c) Dudo que las compre.	*I doubt that he will buy them.*
No creo que tenga dinero.	*I don't believe that he has any money.*
Es posible que lo haya perdido.	*It is possible that he has lost it.*

Note that the indicative is used when there is no doubt in the speaker's mind.

No dudo que las comprará.	*I do not doubt that he will buy them.*
Creo que tiene dinero.	*I believe that he has money.*
Estoy seguro de que no lo ha perdido.	*I am sure he has not lost it.*

109. The Infinitive after Verbs of Command or Permission

After **hacer, mandar,** and **dejar,** the infinitive is more common than the subjunctive, even when the dependent verb has a different subject.

Le hago callar.	*I make him keep silent.*
Me manda hacerlo.	*He orders me to do it.*
Su amo no le deja hablar.	*His master doesn't allow him to speak.*

Exercises

A. *Answer in Spanish.* 1. ¿Por qué camino andan el tío Paco y el tío Pepe? 2. ¿Hace frío? 3. ¿Cuál de los dos acaba de cumplir sesenta y seis años? 4. ¿Por qué no andan con paso rápido? 5. ¿Cuánto tiempo hace que Paco sirve a don Carlos? 6. ¿Dónde tiene casas don Carlos? 7. ¿Vive solo el tío Paco? 8. ¿Cuánto dinero guarda cada mes? 9. ¿ Cuál de los viejecitos tiene su propia casa? 10. ¿Por qué no trabaja todas sus tierras? 11. ¿Qué quiere que haga su amigo? 12. De pronto, ¿qué hace el tío Paco? 13. ¿Qué siente Paco? 14. ¿Cómo tiene los pies? 15. ¿Por qué quiere Pepe que Dios le ayude a Paco? 16. ¿Desea Paco seguir a Pepe o volver a casa? 17. Según Paco, ¿cuándo podría Pepe mostrarle las tierras? 18. Según Paco, ¿qué clase de tierras son? 19. ¿Qué dice de ellas el amo de Paco? 20. ¿Por qué lo dice?

B. *Translate.* 1. Joe does not wish to buy the house. 2. He wants Frank to buy it. 3. Tell him not to do it. 4. It is necessary to see it. 5. It is necessary that you see it. 6. Allow John to see it (*subj.*). 7. He does not allow me to see it (*inf.*). 8. He orders me to guard the animals. 9. It is possible that the lands are not worth a thousand dollars. 10. I doubt that he will offer them to you. 11. I fear that Uncle Frank is sick. 12. I regret that you have not seen him. 13. They fear that he has broken his arm.

C. *Write a synopsis of each of the following* (*present, imperfect, preterit, future, conditional, present subjunctive*). 1. coger (*1st sing.*) 2. comenzar (*1st sing.*) 3. ofrecer (*1st sing; see* § 67) 4. mover (*3d sing.*) 5. producir (*1st sing.*)

D. *Translate.* 1. I stop to look at the horses. 2. Uncle Frank is guarding them. 3 He is sitting on a stone near the river. 4. The sun is shining and it is very warm. 5. "Do you wish me to show you the horses?" asks Uncle Frank. 6. I can catch the black [one] easily. 7. We make our way toward the beautiful animal. 8. The black one doesn't move, but the rest flee. 9. Give him some bread, since you haven't anything else. 10. I fear that he will not eat it. 11. It is possible that he doesn't like stale bread. 12. It doesn't matter that the bread is stale. 13. Uncle Frank has just reached his seventieth birthday. 14. In spite of this, he walks with a rapid step. 15. Uncle Frank's wife does not enjoy good health. 16. She doesn't have strength to accompany her husband. 17. Besides, the horses fear her. 18. Uncle Frank has a horse of his own. 19. His employer has some lands on the other side of the river. 20. If you wish to see them, it will be necessary for you to come with me now. 21. Those lands do not produce much. 22. I regret that he has bought them. 23. May God keep you, Uncle Frank! 24. Good-by sir, I hope that you will come again. 25. I shall return to Córdoba during the afternoon. 26. It is possible that my brother has arrived.

Vocabulary

NOUNS

el **amo,** master, employer
el **calor,** heat
Dios, God
el **esposo,** husband; la esposa, wife
la **fuerza,** force, strength; *pl.*, strength
el **paso,** step, pace
la **piedra,** stone
el **sol,** sun

ADJECTIVES

posible, possible
preciso -a, necessary
propio -a, one's own, private
solo -a, alone, single

VERBS

coger, to seize, catch
comenzar (ie), to commence, begin

cumplir, to fulfill
detener, to detain, stop; **detenerse,** to stop (*intransitive*)
dudar, to doubt
guardar, to guard, keep, save
mostrar (ue), to show
mover (ue), to move; **moverse, to** move (*intransitive*)
ofrecer, to offer
producir, to produce
temer, to fear

ADVERBS

durante, during
además, besides

OPTIONAL VOCABULARY

hace frío, it is cold
hace buen (mal) tiempo, the
  weather is good (bad)
llover (ue), to rain

la lluvia, rain
  nevar (ie), to snow
la nieve, snow
el viento, wind; hace viento, it is
  windy

Refrán

A la necesidad no hay ley.
Necessity knows no law.

*learn forms of
imperfect only*

*1 0 minute quiz over this
chapter 21*

Lección Veintidós

IDIOMS

buenas tardes, good afternoon
cumplir con (su) palabra, to keep (his, her, your) promise, word
en cuanto, as soon as
en fin, in short
en vez de, instead of
por completo, completely
por supuesto, of course

— Buenas tardes, Carlos, ¿qué hace Vd. ahí?

— Acabo de leer lo que dijo don Quijote a Sancho Panza en cierta ocasión. Vd. recordará que Sancho, en varias ocasiones, quería volver a su casa a trabajar sus tierras, en vez de servir a don Quijote. A veces, el deseo de tener una isla era la única cosa que le hacía seguir a su amo. Ahora, iba a recibir la isla; por lo menos, así creía. Ya no habría necesidad de trabajar; tendría mucho dinero. Le engañaban, por supuesto, pero el pobre Sancho no se daba cuenta de eso. No iban a enviarle a una isla, sino a un pueblo, puesto que no existía la isla de que le hablaban. Se disponía para el viaje e iba a partir aquella misma tarde. Supongo que Vd. recuerda la ocasión.

— Sí, recuerdo la ocasión, pero he olvidado casi por completo lo que don Quijote le dijo aquel día. Sé, sin embargo, que sus palabras no eran las de un loco, sino de un santo. Por lo menos, así me parecieron al leerlas por primera vez. Don Quijote llevó aparte a Sancho, para poder hablarle en secreto, ¿no es verdad?

— Sí. Le habló primero de las cosas del espíritu; es decir, de las cosas del alma. Luego, le habló de las cosas del cuerpo; es decir, de cómo había de vestirse; de lo que había de comer y beber; en fin, de las cosas que tocan a la salud.

— ¡Ya recuerdo! Le dijo que tuviese fe en Dios. Le mandó que siempre procurara descubrir la verdad, para que pudiera tratar con justicia a todo el mundo. Le dijo que no comiese mucho y que no bebiese mucho. Le advirtió que el vino "ni guarda secreto ni cumple palabra." [1]

— ¡Hombre, qué memoria! A Vd. le gusta el *Quijote*, ¿verdad?

— Muchísimo. No hay libro que me guste más. Pero, dejemos aparte al *Quijote*, Carlos. Deseo hablarle de otra cosa. Necesito un hombre que me ayude a escribir una carta en francés. En mi casa no hay nadie que sepa el francés. [2] ¿Podría ayudarme su hermano?

— Creo que sí. Se lo preguntaré cuando vuelva.

— ¿Dónde está?

— No sé. Salió esta mañana, sin que nadie le viese. En cuanto vuelva, aunque sea tarde, le enviaré a su casa.

— Mil gracias, Miguel.

— De nada.

110. The Imperfect Subjunctive

The imperfect subjunctive has two sets of endings for -ar verbs and two for -er and -ir verbs.

---

[1] **ni cumple palabra**, *nor keeps a promise*. In modern Spanish, the idiom is usually **cumplir con (su) palabra**, *to keep (his, her, your) promise*.

[2] The definite article is generally used with the name of a language. It is omitted after the prepositions **de** and **en**, after **hablar**, and usually after such verbs as **escribir, estudiar,** and **aprender**.

cantar

cantase	cantásemos		cantara	cantáramos
cantases	cantaseis	or	cantaras	cantarais
cantase	cantasen		cantara	cantaran

comer

comiese	comiésemos		comiera	comiéramos
comieses	comieseis	or	comieras	comierais
comiese	comiesen		comiera	comieran

111. Imperfect Subjunctive of Irregular Verbs

In the imperfect subjunctive, all irregular verbs take the stem of the third person plural preterit.

poder

pudiese	pudiésemos		pudiera	pudiéramos
pudieses	pudieseis	or	pudieras	pudierais
pudiese	pudiesen		pudiera	pudieran

ir and ser

fuese [1]	fuésemos		fuera [1]	fuéramos
fueses	fueseis	or	fueras	fuerais
fuese	fuesen		fuera	fueran

112. The Past Perfect (Pluperfect) Subjunctive

The past perfect subjunctive is formed with the imperfect subjunctive of **haber** and a past participle.

hubiese hablado, etc.   hubiera hablado, etc.

113. Sequence of Tenses

The usual sequence of tenses is indicated by the following table.

---

[1] When the **i** of the preterit ending (-**ieron**) is dropped, it is also dropped in the imperfect subjunctive. Other examples: (decir) **dijese, dijera;** (traer) **trajese, trajera;** (conducir) **condujese, condujera.**

VERB OF MAIN CLAUSE	VERB OF DEPENDENT CLAUSE
Present indicative Future indicative Command form	Present or present perfect sub-junctive [1]
Any past tense of the indicative Conditional	·Imperfect or past perfect sub-junctive

114. Subjunctive in Adjective and Adverb Clauses

The subjunctive is used in adjective (relative) clauses when the antecedent is *indefinite* or *nonexistent*.

Necesito un hombre que me ayude.   *I need a man to help me.*

Aquí no hay nadie que sepa el francés.   *Here there is no one who knows French.*

No hay libro que me guste más.   *There is no book that I like more.*

The subjunctive is used in adverb clauses to express (1) *purpose*, (2) *negative result*, (3) *a future event* or *state*, and (4) *concession*. Purpose clauses are generally introduced by **para que**, negative result by **sin que**, a future event or state by **cuando, en cuanto,** or **hasta que,** and concession by **aunque.**

(1) Se lo digo a Vd., para que sepa la verdad.   *I am telling you, in order that you may know the truth.*

Le mandó que siempre procurara descubrir la verdad, para que pudiera tratar con justicia a todo el mundo.   *He ordered him to try always to discover the truth, in order that he might treat everybody justly.*

(2) Salió esta mañana, sin que nadie le viese.   *He left this morning, without anyone's seeing him.*

La puerta se abre, sin que nadie la toque.   *The door opens, without anybody's touching it.*

(3) En cuanto vuelva, se lo preguntaré.   *As soon as he returns, I shall ask him.*

---

[1] The present tense of a verb like **sentir (dudar, creer)** may be followed by a past tense of the subjunctive. **Siento que Vd. no estuviera allí.** *I regret that you were not there.* **Dudo que hubiera llegado.** *I doubt that he had arrived.*

Lo hará cuando Vd. quiera.   *He will do it whenever you wish.*

(4) Aunque sea tarde, le enviaré a   *Even if it is late, I shall send him*
su casa.   *to your house.*

No lo comprará, aunque tenga   *He won't buy it, even if he has*
dinero.[1]   *money.*

Exercises

A. *Answer in Spanish.* 1. ¿Qué acaba de leer Carlos? 2. ¿Qué quería hacer Sancho en varias ocasiones? 3. ¿Qué le hacía seguir a su amo? 4. ¿Qué creía Sancho? 5. ¿De qué no se daba cuenta? 6. ¿Por qué no iban a enviarle a la isla? 7. ¿Para qué se disponía Sancho? 8. ¿Cuándo iba a partir? 9. ¿Qué había olvidado Miguel? 10. Al leer por primera vez las palabras de don Quijote, ¿cómo le parecieron a Miguel? 11. ¿Qué hizo don Quijote para poder hablar en secreto a Sancho Panza? 12. ¿De qué le habló primero? 13. Y luego, ¿de qué le habló? 14. ¿Qué le mandó hacer para que pudiera tratar con justicia a todos? 15. En cuanto al vino, ¿qué le advirtió? 16. ¿Le gusta a Miguel el *Quijote?* 17. ¿Qué necesita Miguel? 18. ¿Quién podría ayudarle? 19. ¿Cuándo se lo preguntará Carlos? 20. ¿Por qué no sabe Carlos dónde está su hermano?

B. *Write synopses (present, imperfect, preterit, future, conditional, present subjunctive, imperfect subjunctive).* 1. enviar[2] (*3d sing.*) 2. existir (*3d pl.*) 3. partir (*1st sing.*) 4. recordar (*1st sing.*) 5. suponer (*1st sing.*) 6. tocar (*1st sing.*)

C. *Complete the following, using the correct forms of the verbs given in parentheses, and translate.* 1. ¿Desea Vd. que le (mostrar) otra cosa? 2. Temo que Juan no (venir). 3. Temía que Juan no (venir). 4. Espero que ellos no (llegar). 5. Esperaba que Carlos me las (traer). 6. Siento que no (existir) la isla. 7. Sentí que

---

[1] If the concessive clause states a fact, the indicative is used. **No lo compró, aunque tenía dinero.** *He did not buy it, although he had money.*

[2] In the present tense (indicative and subjunctive), **enviar** has an accented **i**, except in the first and second persons plural. **envío, envías,** etc. See § 132, No. 12.

Pepe no me lo (decir). 8. Es preciso que Vd. (tener) dinero. 9. Era preciso que ellos (tener) dinero. 10. No hay nadie que (atreverse) a tocarlo. 11. Busco a alguien que me (enseñar) el francés. 12. Voy a traerlo, para que Vd. lo (ver). 13. Lo traje, para que Juan lo (ver). 14. Partió sin que su padre lo (saber). 15. Se lo diré en cuanto (salir) Carlos. 16. Se lo daré a Vd. cuando lo (pagar). 17. Espero que (venir) Contreras, aunque no (cantar). 18. Me quedo aquí hasta que Vd. me (llamar). 19. Haga Vd. el favor de no salir hasta que yo (volver).

D. *Translate.* 1. Have you ordered the bread and the meat, Anthony? 2. Mr. López said he would send them as soon as he could. 3. Mr. López always keeps his word, doesn't he? 4. Of course, but there isn't anyone who doesn't forget at times. 5. The man does not exist who can say that he never forgets anything. 6. On a certain occasion, Uncle Frank couldn't remember his own name. 7. It was St. John's day and he had drunk a lot of wine. 8. Yes, he had lost his head completely. 9. Charles and Michael were getting ready to go to the country. 10. They were going to spend the day on an island. 11. They hoped that Joe would accompany them. 12. Charles wanted Michael to send the servant to Joe's house. 13. They needed someone to tell him, in order that he might not be (arrive) late. 14. They feared that Joe had forgotten the hour. 15. It was three o'clock and they were to leave within half an hour. 16. Suddenly the door opened and Joe entered the room. 17. Now the only thing they lacked was the meat. 18. The servant called Michael aside to tell him that the meat had arrived. 19. An hour later the servant discovered that the boys had left the bread on the table. 20. He realized, of course, that they would need it. 21. They would not be able to buy bread on the island, even if they had money. 22. "It is possible that my employer will not allow me to take it to them," he thought. 23. But there wasn't time to ask him. 24. In short, Anthony seized the bread and left without anybody's knowing it.

Vocabulary

NOUNS

el deseo, desire
el espíritu, spirit
la fe, faith
la isla, island
la necesidad, necessity, need
la ocasión, occasion
el santo [1] (la santa), saint

ADJECTIVES

cierto -a, certain; a certain
completo -a, complete
único -a, only, unique

VERBS

descubrir, to discover
disponer, to arrange, prepare;
  disponerse, to get ready
enviar, to send
existir, to exist
necesitar, to need
partir, to depart
recordar (ue), to remember

suponer, to suppose
tocar, to touch; to concern

ADVERBS

aparte, aside
luego, then, afterward

CONJUNCTION

e, and (before a word beginning with
  i or hi)

OPTIONAL VOCABULARY

despedirse de, to say good-by to,
  take leave of; se despidió de
  nosotros, he said good-by to us
hasta luego, good-by, so long
tocar la guitarra (el piano), to
  play the guitar (the piano);
  tocarle a uno, to be one's turn;
  ahora me toca a mí, now it is
  my turn

Refrán

Aunque la mona se vista de seda, mona se queda.
Though the monkey dress in silk, she is still a monkey (Dress a
monkey as you will, it remains a monkey still).

---

[1] The final syllable -to is dropped before the names of saints, except those beginning with to or do. San Juan, San Pablo, etc., but Santo Tomás, Santo Domingo.

Lección Veintitrés

IDIOMS

de otro modo, otherwise
pensar en, to think about
referirse a, to refer to

— Veo que Vd. está escribiendo, Luis. ¿Quiere Vd. que quite esos papeles, para que tenga más espacio en la mesa?

— Mil gracias, Miguel, y haga el favor de entregarme el más grande de esos libros, el que trata de ciencias naturales. Fué escrito por un antiguo amigo de mi padre.

— Vd. se refiere a don José Gómez, ¿verdad?

— Sí, a él me refiero. Estaba pensando en don José cuando Vd. entró.

— Dicen que era persona de muchísimo valor. ¿Le recuerda Vd., Luis?

— Por supuesto. Siendo niño, le veía muchas veces. Venía a hablar con mi padre de la ciencia. Don José tenía esperanzas de ser otro Ramón y Cajal.[1] Aunque jamás llegó a ser un gran hombre de ciencia, siempre tenía la cabeza llena de pensamientos profundos. Era el honor y la gloria de nuestro pueblo.

— ¿Qué cosas de valor fueron descubiertas por don José, Luis?

[1] Santiago Ramón y Cajal (1852–1934), biologist, recipient of a Nobel prize (1906), known throughout the world for his studies on the nervous system.

— En cuanto a eso, no puedo decirle nada. Pregúnteselo a mi padre. Lo que puedo decir es que don José solía pasar el día entero leyendo y escribiendo. Su único placer era el de trabajar. Espero que Dios le haya dado un lugar en el cielo donde pueda seguir escribiendo. De otro modo, no será feliz.

— ¿Vive aún su esposa, doña María?

— La pobre mujer murió hace tres años. Durante sus últimos días no gozaba de buena salud. Además, tenía los ojos muy malos, tan malos que apenas podía distinguir el día de la noche. Sufría mucho, y nunca dejó de llorar la muerte de su marido.

— Dicen que doña María no comprendía las ideas de don José.

— Es posible que tengan razón. En cuanto a los libros, no leía mucho, y no podía distinguir lo bueno de lo malo. Le gustaba más hablar que leer, y lo peor era que repetía mil veces las mismas cosas. Sin embargo, era mujer de sentimientos nobles y de buena voluntad para todo el mundo.

115. The Present Participle

The present participle is formed by adding **-ando** to the stem of **-ar** verbs and **-iendo** to the stem of **-er** and **-ir** verbs. The present participle is invariable (always ends in **-o**).

hablar, *to speak*	**hablando,** *speaking*	
comer, *to eat*	**comiendo,** *eating*	
vivir, *to live*	**viviendo,** *living*	

The present participle of **-ir** radical-changing verbs has the same stem as the third person plural preterit.

sentir, *to feel*	**sintiendo,** *feeling*	
servir, *to serve*	**sirviendo,** *serving*	
dormir, *to sleep*	**durmiendo,** *sleeping*	

The present participle of the following verbs must be learned separately. Remember that **i** changes to **y** between two vowels, unless accented.

poder,	*to be able*	pudiendo,	*being able*
decir,	*to say*	diciendo,	*saying*
ir,	*to go*	yendo,	*going*
venir,	*to come*	viniendo,	*coming*
caer,	*to fall*	cayendo,	*falling*
creer,	*to believe*	creyendo,	*believing*
leer,	*to read*	leyendo,	*reading*

116. Uses of the Present Participle

(1) The present participle is used with an auxiliary verb (usually **estar**) [1] to form the progressive tenses. These tenses emphasize the fact that the action is in progress and, therefore, present a more vivid picture.

Están comiendo y bebiendo.	*They are eating and drinking.*
La pobre mujer estaba llorando.	*The poor woman was weeping.*

(2) The present participle is also used to express a variety of adverbial relationships. Keep in mind, however, that the participle is used *without* a preposition.

Leyendo, se aprende mucho.	*By reading, one learns much (much is learned).*
Siendo niño, le veía muchas veces.	*When I was a child, I used to see him often.*

117. Position of Object Pronouns with the Present Participle

When used with a progressive tense, the object pronoun may either follow the participle or precede the auxiliary verb. It is more likely to precede when the auxiliary is **estar.**

La está mirando *or* Está mirándola.	*He is looking at her.*
Sigue sirviéndome.	*He continues to serve me.* [2]
Me dijo que siguiese leyendo.	*He told me to keep on reading.*

---

[1] Other common auxiliaries are **andar, ir,** and **venir. Pepe iba recogiendo los papeles.** *Joe was picking up the papers.*

[2] The present participle (not the infinitive) is always used after **seguir.**

118. The Passive Voice with *ser*

The passive voice, especially when the agent is expressed, is formed as in English, with the verb *to be* (ser) and the past participle. The past participle agrees with the subject in gender and number. The agent is generally introduced by **por**. (Review § 93.)

Cosas de gran valor fueron descubiertas por él.	*Things of great value were discovered by him.*
El libro fué escrito por Ramón y Cajal.	*The book was written by Ramón y Cajal.*
La ventana fué abierta por el criado.	*The window was opened by the servant.*

119. The Neuter Article

The neuter article **lo**, *the*, cannot be used with nouns, since there are no neuter nouns in Spanish. Its principal use is with adjectives. When so used, the adjective is nearly the equivalent of an abstract noun.

No podía distinguir lo bueno de lo malo.	*She could not distinguish the good from the bad.*
Lo peor era que repetía mil veces las mismas cosas.	*The worst (of it) was that she repeated the same things a thousand times.*

Exercises

A. *Answer in Spanish.* 1. ¿Estaba hablando Luis cuando Miguel entró? 2. ¿Qué hizo Miguel, para que Luis tuviera más espacio en la mesa? 3. Luego, ¿qué hizo Miguel? 4. ¿Por quién fué escrito el libro? 5. ¿Qué clase de persona era don José? 6. ¿De qué solían hablar don José y el padre de Luis? 7. ¿Qué esperanzas tenía don José? 8. ¿De qué tenía llena la cabeza? 9. ¿Qué preguntó Miguel a Luis? 10. ¿Cómo respondió Luis? 11. ¿Cómo solía pasar el día don José? 12. ¿Qué esperaba Luis que Dios le hubiera dado? 13. Según Luis, ¿qué necesitaría don José para ser feliz? 14. ¿Cuánto tiempo hace que murió doña María? 15. ¿Cómo tenía los ojos durante sus últimos días? 16. ¿Qué no podía distinguir apenas? 17. ¿Llora Vd. muchas veces? 18. En cuanto a los libros, ¿qué no podía distinguir doña María? 19. ¿Qué solía repetir ella? 20. ¿Qué clase de mujer era doña María?

B. *Translate, using the progressive tenses.* 1. He is writing to me. 2. They were speaking to us. 3. He was sleeping. 4. Are they serving the same master? 5. John is probably reading. 6. We are suffering. 7. The child is taking off her dress. 8. Joe was repeating the words.

C. *Write synopses of the following verbs (all simple tenses of the indicative and subjunctive).* 1. distinguir (*1st sing.*) 2. entregar (*1st sing.*) 3. referir (*3d sing.*) 4. repetir (*3d pl.*)

D. *Translate.* 1. Do you know Mrs. Marco's husband? 2. I have not had the honor of meeting him. 3. Why do you ask me? 4. Well, I was reading one of his works when you entered. 5. It is full of profound thoughts and noble sentiments. 6. I like especially the parts that treat of science. 7. When you were (*pres. part.*) a child, you didn't like science. 8. You used (were accustomed) to weep when you had to read such books. 9. In spite of that, those were the happiest days of my life. 10. It was not my own will but that of my father that made me work. 11. Seeing me remove my eyes from the book, he would (used to) tell me to keep on reading. 12. Otherwise, he thought, I would never get to be a distinguished man. 13. But at last he lost all hope. 14. The bad part of it was that he suffered more than I. 15. By the way, is your aunt still living? 16. As they say in Spanish, she delivered her soul to God four years ago. 17. During the space of six months before her death, she could hardly move her hand. 18. The glories of this world did not matter to her. 19. To what glories do you refer? 20. Don't you know that she was presented to the king?

Vocabulary

NOUNS

el **cielo**, heaven; sky
la **ciencia**, science
el **espacio**, space, room
la **esperanza**, hope
la **gloria**, glory
el **honor**, honor
el **marido**, husband
la **mujer**, woman, wife
el **pensamiento**, thought
el **sentimiento**, sentiment, feeling
el **valor**, value, worth
la **voluntad**, will

ADJECTIVES

feliz, happy (*used with* **ser**)
noble, noble
profundo, profound, deep

VERBS

distinguir, to distinguish
entregar, to deliver; to hand (over)
llorar, to weep (over)
quitar, to remove; **quitarse**, to take off
referir (ie), to refer
repetir (i), to repeat
soler (ue), to be accustomed
sufrir, to suffer

OPTIONAL VOCABULARY

alegrarse (de), to rejoice (at), be glad (of); me **alegro de verle a Vd.**, I am glad to see you
alegre, merry
reír (i), to laugh; **reírse de**, to laugh at (se **ríe de ella**, he laughs at her)

Refrán

A Dios rogando y con el mazo dando.
Pray God, but keep hammering.

Lección Veinticuatro

IDIOMS

al contrario, on the contrary
a la sombra de, in the shade of
de vez en cuando, from time to time
echar a (correr), to start to (run)
en el fondo (del río), at the bottom (of the river)
en sueños, in (one's) dreams
meterse en (el agua), to plunge into (the water)

Eran las nueve de la mañana cuando el tío Pepe entró en la ciudad de Córdoba. Le hacía falta un caballo, y buscaba un animal que fuese joven y fuerte. Cierto vecino suyo ya le había ofrecido uno muy bueno, y si no hubiera sido de color blanco, lo habría comprado. El tío Pepe no compraría un caballo blanco, aunque fuese el mejor animal de España. ¿Por qué? me pregunta Vd. Por lo que le pasó hace tres años. Sucedió de esta manera:

El tío Pepe estaba trabajando en sus tierras con un viejo caballo blanco. Hacía muchísimo calor. A las cuatro de la tarde, estando muy cansado el caballo, el tío Pepe lo puso en libertad, para que fuese a beber al río. Viéndose libre, el pobre animal echó a correr hacia el Guadalquivir y poco después Pepe lo vió bajar al río. El caballo tenía mucho calor y se metió en el agua, sin darse cuenta de que el río en aquel punto era muy profundo.

El tío Pepe se sentó a la sombra de un árbol. Sacó lo poco que le quedaba de la carne que su esposa le había entregado al salir de casa por la mañana. Cortó un pedazo y se puso a comerlo. No comió mucho, sin embargo; al contrario, antes de terminar el último pedazo, los ojos del viejecito se cerraban, y poco después estaba durmiendo profundamente. De vez en cuando, hacía un movimiento rápido de la mano, como si tratase de apartar de sí alguna cosa. Veía en sueños una figura blanca en forma de caballo, pero con cabeza de mujer. Tenía los ojos grandísimos. Al acercarse, los ojos parecían unirse, formando un solo punto de fuego. La luz del fuego era tan fuerte que el tío Pepe apenas podía mirarla. Trató de apartar de ella los ojos y no pudo. Si hubiera podido levantarse, habría huído, pero sus pies se negaban a moverse.

El ojo de fuego era, por supuesto, el sol, pero el tío Pepe no se daba cuenta de eso. Al despertarse media hora después, ya no había sol. Se levantó y se dirigió al río. ¿Dónde estaba el caballo? Más de dos horas lo buscó el tío Pepe. Una vez creyó ver, en el fondo del río, un cuerpo blanco. ¿Había bajado por las aguas, como si fuera una piedra? No, eso no; era imposible. En cambio, no halló nada que indicara que el animal hubiera salido del río.

El tío Pepe estaba muy triste. Además, tenía dolor de cabeza. Sentándose en el suelo, puso los ojos en las aguas profundas y obscuras. De pronto, creyó oír la voz de una mujer. Era una voz baja y dulce, y parecía salir de lo más profundo del río. A veces la mujer parecía estar llorando.

"Será alma en pena," dijo el tío Pepe. "¡Si los caballos tuviesen alma, . . .! No, el mío habrá vuelto a casa mientras yo dormía."

Sin embargo, el caballo no había vuelto a casa, y el tío Pepe no volvió a verle jamás.

120. Subjunctive in Conditional Sentences

An if-clause expressing (1) *uncertainty* or (2) a *condition contrary to fact* requires the imperfect or pluperfect subjunctive. The result clause takes the conditional or the conditional perfect.

(1) Si me ofreciese (ofreciera) el caballo, lo compraría.	*If he should offer me the horse, I would buy it.*
Si viniera, se lo diría.	*If he should come, I would tell him.*
(2) Si tuviese dinero, lo compraría.	*If I had money, I would buy it.*
Si no hubiera sido de color blanco, lo habría comprado.	*If it had not been white, he would have bought it.*
Si hubiera podido levantarse, habría huído.	*If he had been able to get up, he would have fled.*

121. Subjunctive after *como si*

Clauses introduced by **como si,** *as if,* are like the if-clauses of contrary-to-fact conditions.

¿Había bajado por las aguas, como si fuera una piedra?	*Had it gone down through the water, as if it were a stone?*
De vez en cuando, hacía un movimiento rápido de la mano, como si tratase de apartar de sí alguna cosa.	*From time to time he made a quick movement of the hand, as if he were trying to push something away (from himself).*
Siguió escribiendo, como si no hubiera sucedido nada.	*He kept on writing, as if nothing had happened.*

122. If-Clauses without Subjunctive

When the if-clause does not express uncertainty or a condition contrary to fact, the indicative is used. Remember that **si,** *if,* is never followed by the *present* subjunctive.

Si tiene dinero, me lo da.	*If he has money, he gives it to me.*
Si tenía dinero, no lo sabía su padre.	*If he had money. his father didn't know it.*

Exercises

A. *Answer in Spanish.* 1. ¿Qué le hacía falta al tío Pepe? 2. ¿Qué clase de caballo buscaba? 3. ¿Por qué no había comprado el que le ofreció su vecino? 4. ¿Hace cuántos años que sucedió lo que pasa en el cuento? 5. ¿Qué hacía el tío Pepe aquella tarde?

6. ¿Por qué puso en libertad a su caballo? 7. Viéndose libre, ¿qué hizo el caballo? 8. ¿Por qué se metió en el agua? 9. ¿De qué no se dió cuenta el caballo? 10. ¿Dónde se sentó el tío Pepe? 11. ¿Qué hizo después de sentarse? 12. ¿Por qué no comió mucho? 13. Mientras dormía, ¿qué hacía de vez en cuando? 14. ¿Qué veía en sueños? 15. ¿Qué clase de ojos tenía la figura? 16. Mientras se acercaba al tío Pepe, ¿qué hacían los ojos? 17. Si hubiera podido levantarse, ¿qué habría hecho el tío Pepe? 18. Al despertarse, ¿qué hizo? 19. ¿Qué hizo durante más de dos horas? 20. ¿Qué creyó ver en el fondo del río? 21. Después de sentarse en el suelo, ¿qué hizo? 22. De pronto, ¿qué creyó oír? 23. ¿Hablaba o lloraba la mujer? 24. ¿Le parece a Vd. que era una voz o el agua lo que oía el pobre viejo?

B. *Translate the words in italics, then translate the completed sentence into English.* 1. Si Vd. me *would cut* un pedazo de carne, lo *I would eat.* 2. Si el caballo no *had been* blanco, Pepe lo *would have bought.* 3. Si *she should need* un vestido, su padre se lo *would give.* 4. Si *you* me lo *had told*, no lo *I would have believed.* 5. *He would refuse* comprarlo, aunque *he had* dinero. 6. Si *they should approach* a la casa, los *he would kill.* 7. Si *it is* frío, no *we shall go.* 8. Si *he received* el dinero, su carta *does not indicate it.*

C. *Translate.* 1. He approaches me. 2. I approach him. 3. Push those things aside. 4. Cut the bread. 5. Joe wakes up. 6. Joe, wake up. 7. What does that indicate? 8. Put it in your mouth. 9. He plunges into the water. 10. I deny that he is (*subj.*)[1] here. 11. It happened last night. 12. Here the two rivers unite, forming one.

D. *Translate.* 1. John was walking along the road under the trees. 2. He feared that the night would be dark. 3. The only light came from a house on the other side of the river. 4. From time to time he saw little animals. 5. On seeing John, they

---

[1] The subjunctive regularly follows an expression of denial.

plunged into the shadows. 6. Once John thought he saw [1] the figure of a man. 7. He was coming through the fields toward the road. 8. John could see the movement of his arms. 9. Suddenly he realized that the man was no longer there. 10. The boy refused to believe that his eyes had deceived him. 11. I deny that he had seen anybody. 12. Did John stop to look for the man? 13. On the contrary, he started to run. 14. He remembered what had happened there a month before. 15. There Uncle Joe had lost his horse. 16. In his dreams the old man still hears that sweet voice. 17. I mean the voice that seemed to come out of the deepest part of the river. 18. They say that the body of the horse was found at the bottom of the river. 19. If they had found it, they would have told Uncle Joe. 20. He used to talk to that horse, as if it were a person.

Vocabulary

NOUNS

la figura, figure
el fondo, bottom
la forma, form
la libertad, liberty
la luz, light
el movimiento, movement
el pedazo, piece
la pena, grief, distress
la sombra, shade, shadow

PRONOUN

sí (reflex. obj. of a prep.), himself, herself, itself, themselves

VERBS

acercarse (a), to approach
apartar, to push aside or away
cortar, to cut
despertar (ie), to awaken; despertarse, to wake up
indicar, to indicate
meter, to put in
negar (ie), to deny; negarse a, to refuse
suceder, to happen
unir, to join, unite; unirse, to unite

PREPOSITION

hacia, toward

---

[1] Use the infinitive. This is the usual construction when the subject of the dependent infinitive is the same as that of the main verb.

ADJECTIVES	OPTIONAL VOCABULARY
bajo -a, low	**figurarse,** to imagine; **se figura**
contrario -a, contrary	**que va a ganar,** he imagines
dulce, sweet	that he is going to win
libre, free	**reunirse,** to meet, get together;
obscuro -a, dark	**se reunen aquí,** they meet here

Quien espera, desespera;	He who waits, despairs; (but)
Quien desespera, no alcanza;	He who despairs, does not attain;
Por eso es bueno esperar . . .	Therefore 'tis well to wait . . .
Y no perder la esperanza.	And not give up hope.

Lección Veinticinco

IDIOMS

acababa de (comprarle), had just (bought him)
al día siguiente, on the following day
allá voy, I'm coming
el lunes, on Monday
en todo caso, in any case; anyhow
momentos después, a few moments later
respecto a, with regard to
sin duda, doubtless; **sin duda alguna**, without any doubt
(tres veces) al día, (three times) a day
(vamos) a ver, let's see

En un pueblo del estado de Pennsylvania vive un antiguo amigo de Carlos. Se llama Joseph White. El lunes pasado Carlos fué a verle en el automóvil que su padre acababa de comprarle. Salió de Nueva York a las siete de la mañana. Todos los caminos estaban en buenas condiciones [1] y el automóvil andaba bien, de manera que pudo hacer el viaje en seis horas. Al día siguiente, Joseph volvió con él a Nueva York y ahora los encontramos en casa de Miguel. Están hablando de la literatura española. Joseph conoce bastante bien los autores del Siglo de Oro.[2] Ha estudiado un año en la Habana y dos años en Madrid.

---

[1] *in good condition.* Note use of plural.
[2] *the Golden Age* of Spanish literature (about 1550–1650).

— Dime, José, ¿cuántas obras escribió Lope de Vega? [1]

— Respecto al número de sus obras, no puedo decírtelo, Carlos. Se dice que escribió mil ochocientas.

— ¡Parece imposible! Para escribir tantos libros un hombre tendría que vivir más de cien años.

— Sí, parece imposible, y yo no creo que Lope escribiese mil ochocientos; pero, en todo caso, el número es muy grande.

— ¿Y has leído tú todos esos libros?

— Nadie puede leerlos todos, puesto que la mayor parte de ellos se han perdido.

— ¿Cuántos se conservan?

— Unos cuatrocientos cincuenta, todos dignos de estudio. Yo, al término de mis estudios en Madrid, no había podido leer más que sesenta, porque Lope no era el único autor del Siglo de Oro cuyas obras estudiamos. Pasé muchas horas leyendo las obras de Calderón [2] y las de Cervantes. Como poeta me gusta más Calderón que Lope. No escribió tanto; en cambio, escribió con más cuidado. Por supuesto el que me gusta más es Cervantes. Ocupa, sin duda alguna, el primer puesto en la literatura española.

— Basta de literatura, amigos. Quizá no sepáis [3] que son cerca de las ocho y no hemos comido todavía. Permitidme deciros que es preciso conservar la buena costumbre de comer lo menos tres veces al día. El pan y el vino valen mucho más que cualquier libro.

— Habla con más respeto, Luis. De vez en cuando debes poner los pensamientos en las cosas del espíritu. Tienes buena cabeza, pero no quieres usarla.

— Lo que quiero emplear ahora no es la cabeza, sino los pies.

— ¿Para qué quieres emplearlos?

— Para ir a un café a comer. Ya es tarde para comer en casa. Vámonos.

---

[1] Lope de Vega Carpio, Spanish dramatist (1562–1635).

[2] Pedro Calderón de la Barca, Spanish dramatist (1600–1681).

[3] The subjunctive is used after quizá (tal vez), *perhaps*, when there is strong doubt in the mind of the speaker.

— Un momento.   No están presentes todos nuestros compañeros.   Vamos a ver si Miguel está en su cuarto.

— No está en su cuarto.   Salió hace un momento.   ¡Antonio, ven acá!

— Allá voy, señorito.

— A ver si puedes alcanzar a Miguel.   Acaba de salir.

(*Momentos después vuelve el criado acompañado de Miguel y los amigos salen juntos a la calle.*)

— ¿A qué café quieres ir, Luis?

— A cualquiera.

— Pues entonces vamos al Café Español.

123. The Imperative

The imperative is used to express an affirmative command when the person is addressed as **tú** (*pl.*, **vosotros**).   The singular of the imperative is generally the same as the third person singular present indicative.   The plural, without exception, is the same as the infinitive with the final **r** changed to **d**.

AFFIRMATIVE COMMAND (imperative)	NEGATIVE COMMAND (subjunctive) [1]
habla (**tú**), *speak*	no **hables** (**tú**), *don't speak*
hablad (**vosotros**), *speak*	no **habléis** (**vosotros**), *don't speak*
come (**tú**), *eat*	no **comas** (**tú**), *don't eat*
comed (**vosotros**), *eat*	no **comáis** (**vosotros**), *don't eat*
ábrela (**tú**), *open it*	no la **abras** (**tú**), *don't open it*
abridla (**vosotros**), *open it*	no la **abráis** (**vosotros**), *don't open it*
ciérrala (**tú**), *close it*	no la **cierres** (**tú**), *don't close it*
cerradla (**vosotros**), *close it*	no la **cerréis** (**vosotros**), *don't close it*

The final **d** of the imperative plural is dropped before the reflexive pronoun **os** is added, except in the case of **irse**.

siéntate, *sit down*	no te **sientes**, *don't sit down*
sentaos, *sit down*	no os **sentéis**, *don't sit down*
idos, *go away*	no os **vayáis**, *don't go away*

---

[1] All negative commands, familiar and formal, are expressed by the subjunctive.

124. Irregular Imperatives

SINGULAR	PLURAL		SINGULAR	PLURAL	
di	decid,	*say, tell*	vete	idos,	*go away*
haz	haced,	*do*	pon	poned,	*put*
sal	salid,	*leave*	ten	tened,	*have, hold*
sé	sed,	*be*	ven	venid,	*come*
ve	id,	*go*			

125. Definite Article with Names of Countries

The definite article forms a part of the names of certain countries. It is used with the name of any country (except **Puerto Rico** and **Costa Rica**) when the name is modified by an adjective.

el Perú,	*Peru*		el Brasil,	*Brazil*
el Paraguay,	*Paraguay*		el Salvador,	*Salvador*
el Uruguay,	*Uruguay*		el Canadá,	*Canada*
el Ecuador,	*Ecuador*		el Japón,	*Japan*
los Estados Unidos,	*the United States*			
la Gran Bretaña,	*Great Britain*			
la España antigua,	*ancient Spain*			

The article is also used with the names of a few cities: **la Habana,** *Havana*; **la Coruña,** *Corunna*.

126. The Possessive Relative Adjective *cuyo*

cuyo (**cuya, cuyos, cuyas**), *whose, of which,* agrees with the thing possessed. It may refer to persons as well as things.

Estas personas, cuyos nombres tengo escritos aquí, son amigos de Miguel Torres.	*These persons, whose names I have written here, are friends of Miguel Torres.*
Allí va la señora de López, cuya hija se casa con don José.	*There goes Mrs. López, whose daughter is going to marry don José.*
No era el único autor cuyas obras estudiamos.	*He was not the only author whose works we studied.*

Exercises

A. *Answer in Spanish.* 1. ¿Dónde vive el amigo de Carlos?
2. ¿Cuándo fué a verle Carlos? 3. ¿Cómo estaban los caminos?
4. ¿Qué hizo Carlos al día siguiente? 5. ¿Dónde se encuentran los
jóvenes ahora? 6. ¿De qué hablan? 7. ¿Qué autores del Siglo de
Oro le gustan más a José? 8. ¿Cuántas obras escribió Lope de
Vega? 9. ¿Cuántas se conservan hoy? 10. ¿Qué dice José de las
obras de Lope? 11. ¿Cuál de los dos poetas le gusta más?
12. ¿Qué autor ocupa el primer puesto en la literatura española?
13. ¿Qué costumbre debe conservarse, según Luis? 14. ¿Qué dice
Luis del pan? 15. Según uno de sus compañeros, ¿qué no quiere
usar Luis? 16. ¿Para qué quiere emplear los pies? 17. ¿Por qué
no salen en seguida los muchachos? 18. ¿Quién alcanza a Miguel?
19. Momentos después, ¿qué sucede? 20. ¿A qué café quiere ir
Luis?

B. *Change the following to the imperative, singular and plural.*
1. tomarlo 2. beberla 3. dármelo 4. irse 5. venir acá 6. ayu-
darnos 7. decírselo 8. hacerlo 9. ponerlo aquí 10. salir en
seguida 11. ser bueno 12. tener cuidado 13. levantarse 14. acostarse

C. *Change the above to negative commands, singular and plural.*

D. *Translate (use familiar forms wherever possible).* 1. Joseph
left for Pittsburgh on Monday. 2. We tried to overtake him.
3. At the end of two hours the automobile refused to go. 4. Neither
the automobile nor the roads were in good condition. 5. A few
moments later we saw a man coming. 6. He offered to take us to a
town near Pittsburgh. 7. He permitted us to spend the night in
his home. 8. John and I occupied the same room. 9. We returned
for (**por**) the automobile on the following day. 10. By the way, I
intend to go to Havana next month. 11. How do you intend to
go, by sea? 12. I can't tell you anything yet with regard to that.
13. In any case, I shall see you again before leaving. 14. Two,
perhaps three, companions of mine are going with me. 15. We are

going to make the trip with the gentleman whose son you met last night. 16. He likes to teach Spanish literature, especially that of the sixteenth century. 17. Doubtless he is a gentleman worthy of respect. 18. Come here. Let's see what you have in your hand. 19. It is one of the works that we use in class. 20. Each one of those who were present yesterday received one of these books. 21. The book treats of the best ways to preserve the health of children. 22. Someone is calling you. 23. Perhaps it is your father. 24. I'm coming, father. Good-by, Louis. 25. When shall we see [1] each other again? 26. Come tomorrow, at any hour.

Vocabulary

NOUNS

el caso, case
el compañero, companion
la condición, condition
la duda, doubt
el estado, state
la Habana, Havana
la literatura, literature
el lunes, Monday
el puesto, place
el respecto, relation (*used only in prepositional phrases*)
el respeto, respect
el siglo, century
el término, end

ADJECTIVES

cualquier(a), any; *pronoun*, cualquiera, anyone
cuyo -a, whose
digno -a, worthy

presente, present
siguiente, following

VERBS

alcanzar, to overtake, reach
conservar, to preserve, keep
emplear, to employ, use
ocupar, to occupy
permitir, to permit
usar, to use

ADVERBS

acá, here
quizá(s), perhaps

OPTIONAL VOCABULARY

rato, short space of time, while; al poco rato, in a little while

---

[1] Use the present tense. The present is often used for the English future, especially in conversation.

Refranes

Antes que te cases mira lo que haces.
Look before you leap.

Haz bien y no mires a quién.
Do good to all.

Repaso

(LESSONS XXI–XXV)

A. *Translate the italicized words.* 1. Doña Ana *seized her husband by the arm.* 2. *She took him aside* para decirle algo. 3. *A few moments later,* ella comenzó a llorar. 4. La pobre mujer *had just received* una carta de su hijo. 5. *As soon as* empezó a leerla, *she became* tan blanca como el papel. 6. Supongo que *you refer to the* hijo que vive en *Havana.* 7. *Of course.* La carta no puede ser de otro, *since* Pepe es *an* [1] *only son.* 8. *You are right.* Lo había olvidado *completely.* 9. Cuando Pepe y yo vivíamos en *Peru* solía verle *from time to time.* 10. Nos encontramos *for the first time on Monday,* dos de abril de 1934. 11. *On the following day* fuimos juntos a Lima. 12. *It was very warm* aquel día. 13. Fuimos al río, *we took off* los vestidos y *we plunged into* el agua. 14. Sentados *in the shade of* un árbol había siete *or* ocho niños. 15. Al acercarnos, *they started to run toward* la ciudad. 16. Uno de ellos *stopped* un instante para mirarnos. 17. Luego, *realizing that* no podría *catch up with* los otros, *he started to weep.* 18. Antes de acostarme anoche, *I was thinking of* aquellos niños. 19. Los veía *several times in my dreams* durante la noche. 20. Supongo que *you didn't see them again* en Lima. 21. *On the contrary,* solía verlos *at least twice a day.* 22. *Otherwise,* no los recordaría hoy. 23. Creo que su hija *is calling you.* 24. *I'm coming,* hija mía. 25. Mi hija *has just reached her fourth birthday.* 26. *Let's see* si Vd. puede decirme *which* de estas niñas *is mine.* 27. *The one who* acaba de decirme *"good afternoon"* es suya *without any doubt.* 28. Pues, ¿*shall we see* [2] *each other* mañana? 29. *With regard to that,* no

---

[1] Omit.   [2] See note 1, p. 152.

puedo decirle nada ahora, pero *in any case* nos veremos pronto.
30. Tengo que *get ready* para el viaje, tengo que comprar la mar
de cosas, *in short*, estaré ocupadísimo *all day*.

B. *Translate the italicized words.* 1. Espero que Paco *knows* el
nombre del caballero *whose* hijas conocimos anoche. 2. Temo que
he hasn't delivered la carta. 3. Le dije *to deliver it to him* en seguida.
4. *Do not touch* esas flores hasta que María *has seen them.* 5. Dé-
jeme *push them aside*, porque quiero usar la mesa. 6. *I repeat*
que Vd. no ha de *move them.* 7. ¿No quiere Vd. que *I put them*
en agua? 8. Naturalmente. Deseo *to keep them* en buen estado.
9. *Try* no romperlas *on putting them* en el agua. 10. Si el agua
were un poco más profunda, *it would be* mejor. 11. El criado
quería *to cut them*, pero *I did not permit him to do it.* [1] 12. A propósito, no creo que *Louis will be present* hoy. 13. *On waking up*
esta mañana me dijo que tenía *a bad headache.* 14. Si *he had not
drunk* tanto café anoche, *he would not have become* malo. 15. *Anyhow*, espero que *he isn't suffering* mucho. 16. Dudo que *it is* el
café. 17. Niego que el café *can* producir tal efecto. 18. Pues, en
cierta ocasión lo mismo *happened to me.* 19. No hay nada que
I like more than el café pero, si *you should offer it to me* ahora, *I
would not drink it.* 20. Eso *does not indicate* que el café *is* malo
para la salud. 21. Mi padre *does not allow* me beberlo. 22. Si
I had known eso, *I would have ordered* vino.

C. *Complete the sentences of* (a) *with a translation of the appro-
priate phrase from* (b). (a) 1. Hemos pasado muchos . . . en
el campo. 2. Los hombres de ciencia son . . . 3. El 24 de junio
es . . . 4. Que no se cumpla su voluntad sino . . . 5. La isla
no parecía tan hermosa . . . 6. Se lo mostraré a Vd. . . .
7. Era . . . y no podíamos ver el camino. 8. El rey le dió un
caballo . . . 9. No hablaban en voz alta, sino . . . 10. En
el fondo del río había . . . 11. Hijo mío, . . . podrías pedir
dinero a tu padre. 12. El pobre no me pidió más que . . .

---

[1] Omit *to do:* . . . **no se lo permití.**

13. Los santos siempre han trabajado sin . . . 14. Los americanos amamos . . . 15. Doña María vive . . . y no creo que
haya mujer más feliz. 16. Todo el trabajo lo hace con . . .

(b) 1. a dark night   2. her own hands   3. worthy of honor
4. any day   5. liberty and justice   6. hope of glory   7. happy [1]
days   8. free of all care   9. many large stones   10. in (a) the light
of the sun   11. the will of God   12. St. John's day   13. a piece of
bread   14. in a low voice   15. in case of necessity   16. of great
value

---

[1] See note 1, p. 54.

Appendix

127. Simple Tenses of Regular Verbs

INFINITIVE

hablar, *to speak*   comer, *to eat*   vivir, *to live*

PRESENT PARTICIPLE

hablando   comiendo   viviendo

PAST PARTICIPLE

hablado   comido   vivido

Indicative Mood

PRESENT

hablo	como	vivo
hablas	comes	vives
habla	come	vive
hablamos	comemos	vivimos
habláis	coméis	vivís
hablan	comen	viven

IMPERFECT

hablaba	comía	vivía
hablabas	comías	vivías
hablaba	comía	vivía
hablábamos	comíamos	vivíamos
hablabais	comíais	vivíais
hablaban	comían	vivían

PRETERIT

hablé	comí	viví
hablaste	comiste	viviste
habló	comió	vivió
hablamos	comimos	vivimos
hablasteis	comisteis	vivisteis
hablaron	comieron	vivieron

FUTURE

hablaré	comeré	viviré
hablarás	comerás	vivirás
hablará	comerá	vivirá
hablaremos	comeremos	viviremos
hablaréis	comeréis	viviréis
hablarán	comerán	vivirán

CONDITIONAL

hablaría	comería	viviría
hablarías	comerías	vivirías
hablaría	comería	viviría
hablaríamos	comeríamos	viviríamos
hablaríais	comeríais	viviríais
hablarían	comerían	vivirían

Imperative Mood

habla	come	vive
hablad	comed	vivid

Subjunctive Mood

PRESENT

hable	coma	viva
hables	comas	vivas
hable	coma	viva

hablemos	comamos	vivamos
habléis	comáis	viváis
hablen	coman	vivan

IMPERFECT (-se)

hablase	comiese	viviese
hablases	comieses	vivieses
hablase	comiese	viviese
hablásemos	comiésemos	viviésemos
hablaseis	comieseis	vivieseis
hablasen	comiesen	viviesen

IMPERFECT (-ra)

hablara	comiera	viviera
hablaras	comieras	vivieras
hablara	comiera	viviera
habláramos	comiéramos	viviéramos
hablarais	comierais	vivierais
hablaran	comieran	vivieran

128. Compound Tenses of Regular Verbs

PERFECT INFINITIVE

haber hablado	haber comido	haber vivido

PERFECT PARTICIPLE

habiendo hablado	habiendo comido	habiendo vivido

Indicative Mood

PRESENT PERFECT

he			
has			
ha			
	hablado	comido	vivido
hemos			
habéis			
han			

PAST PERFECT

había			
habías			
había			
	hablado	comido	vivido
habíamos			
habíais			
habían			

FUTURE PERFECT

habré			
habrás			
habrá			
	hablado	comido	vivido
habremos			
habréis			
habrán			

CONDITIONAL PERFECT

habría			
habrías			
habría			
	hablado	comido	vivido
habríamos			
habríais			
habrían			

Subjunctive Mood

PRESENT PERFECT

haya			
hayas			
haya			
	hablado	comido	vivido
hayamos			
hayáis			
hayan			

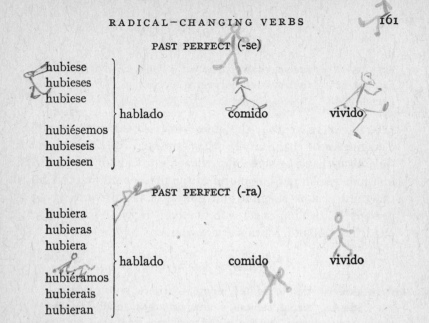

PAST PERFECT (-se)

hubiese
hubieses
hubiese

}

hablado   comido   vivido

hubiésemos
hubieseis
hubiesen

PAST PERFECT (-ra)

hubiera
hubieras
hubiera

}

hablado   comido   vivido

hubiéramos
hubierais
hubieran

129. Radical-Changing Verbs

Stem-vowel **e** becomes **ie** and stem-vowel **o** becomes **ue**, when stressed. All other forms are regular.

cerrar, *to close*

PRES. IND.	**cierro, cierras, cierra,** cerramos, cerráis, **cierran**
PRES. SUBJ.	**cierre, cierres, cierre,** cerremos, cerréis, **cierren**
IMPERATIVE	**cierra,** cerrad

contar, *to count; to tell*

PRES. IND.	**cuento, cuentas, cuenta,** contamos, contáis, **cuentan**
PRES. SUBJ.	**cuente, cuentes, cuente,** contemos, contéis, **cuenten**
IMPERATIVE	**cuenta,** contad

perder, *to lose*

PRES. IND.	**pierdo, pierdes, pierde,** perdemos, perdéis, **pierden**
PRES. SUBJ.	**pierda, pierdas, pierda,** perdamos, perdáis, **pierdan**
IMPERATIVE	**pierde,** perded

volver, *to return*

PRES. IND   **vuelvo, vuelves, vuelve,** volvemos, volvéis, **vuelven**
PRES. SUBJ.   **vuelva, vuelvas, vuelva,** volvamos, volváis, **vuelvan**
IMPERATIVE   **vuelve,** volved

130. As we have seen, the stem vowel of -ar and -er radical-changing verbs changes only when stressed. Note, however, that -ir radical-changing verbs also change e to i and o to u (1) in the first and second persons plural of the present subjunctive, (2) in the third person, singular and plural, of the preterit, (3) in all persons of the imperfect subjunctive, and (4) in the present participle. All other forms are regular.

sentir, *to feel; to regret*

PRES. IND.   **siento, sientes, siente,** sentimos, sentís, **sienten**
PRES. SUBJ.   **sienta, sientas, sienta,** sintamos, sintáis, **sientan**
PRET. IND.   sentí, sentiste, **sintió,** sentimos, sentisteis, **sintieron**
IMP. SUBJ.   **(-se) sintiese, sintieses,** *etc.*
IMP. SUBJ.   **(-ra) sintiera, sintieras,** *etc.*
IMPERATIVE   **siente,** sentid
PRES. PART.   **sintiendo**

morir, *to die*

PRES. IND.   **muero, mueres, muere,** morimos, morís, **mueren**
PRES. SUBJ.   **muera, mueras, muera,** muramos, muráis, **mueran**
PRET. IND.   morí, moriste, **murió,** morimos, moristeis, **murieron**
IMP. SUBJ.   **(-se) muriese, murieses,** *etc.*
IMP. SUBJ.   **(-ra) muriera, murieras,** *etc.*
IMPERATIVE   **muere,** morid
PRES. PART.   **muriendo**

Other verbs of this type: **advertir, referir, dormir.**

131. A few e-stem -ir verbs change e to i, when stressed. All other changes as in **sentir.**

pedir, *to ask (for)*

PRES. IND.	pido, pides, pide, pedimos, pedís, **piden**
PRES. SUBJ.	pida, pidas, pida, pidamos, pidáis, pidan
PRET. IND.	pedí, pediste, pidió, pedimos, pedisteis, pidieron
IMP. SUBJ.	(-se) pidiese, pidieses, *etc.*
IMP. SUBJ.	(-ra) pidiera, pidieras, *etc.*
IMPERATIVE	pide, pedid
PRES. PART.	pidiendo

Other verbs of this type: **repetir, servir**

132. Orthographic-Changing Verbs [1]

1. Verbs in -car

sacar, *to take out*

PRETERIT	saqué, sacaste, *etc.*
PRES. SUBJ.	saque, saques, *etc.*

Other verbs of this type: **acercar, buscar, colocar, tocar.**

2. Verbs in -gar

pagar, *to pay*

PRETERIT	pagué, pagaste, *etc.*
PRES. SUBJ.	pague, pagues, *etc.*

Other verbs of this type: **llegar, negar.**

3. Verbs in -guar

averiguar, *to ascertain*

PRETERIT	averigüé, averiguaste, *etc.*
PRES. SUBJ.	averigüe, averigües, *etc.*

Other verbs of this type: **fraguar,** *to forge;* **menguar,** *to lessen*

---

[1] See § 95.

4. Verbs in -zar

comenzar, *to begin*

PRETERIT   **comencé,** comenzaste, *etc.*
PRES. SUBJ. **comience, comiences,** *etc.*

Other verbs of this type: **alcanzar, gozar.**

5. Verbs in **-cer** and **-cir,** preceded by a consonant.

vencer, *to conquer*

PRES. IND.   **venzo,** vences, *etc.*
PRES. SUBJ. **venza, venzas,** *etc.*

esparcir, *to scatter*

PRES. IND.   **esparzo,** esparces, *etc.*
PRES. SUBJ. **esparza, esparzas,** *etc.*

Other verbs of this type: **torcer (ue),** *to twist;* **uncir,** *to yoke.*

6. Verbs in **-ger** and **-gir**

coger, *to seize*

PRES. IND.   **cojo,** coges, *etc.*
PRES. SUBJ. **coja, cojas,** *etc.*

dirigir, *to direct*

PRES. IND.   **dirijo,** diriges, *etc.*
PRES. SUBJ. **dirija, dirijas,** *etc.*

Other verbs of this type: **corregir (i),** *to correct;* **recoger.**

7. Verbs in **-guir**

seguir, *to follow; to continue*

PRES. IND.   **sigo,** sigues, *etc.*
PRES. SUBJ. **siga, sigas,** *etc.*

Another verb of this type: **distinguir.**

8. Verbs in **-ecer, -ocer,** and **-ucir.**

parecer, *to appear, seem*

PRES. IND.   parezco, pareces, *etc.*
PRES. SUBJ.   **parezca, parezcas,** *etc.*

conocer, *to know*

PRES. IND.   conozco, conoces, *etc.*
PRES. SUBJ.   **conozca, conozcas,** *etc.*

lucir, *to shine*

PRES. IND.   luzco, luces, *etc.*
PRES. SUBJ.   **luzca, luzcas,** *etc.*

Other verbs of this type: **aparecer, conducir, merecer, nacer, ofrecer, producir.**

9. Verbs that change unstressed **i** to **y** between vowels. Note the written accents.

leer, *to read*

PRETERIT   leí, leíste, **leyó,** leímos, leísteis, **leyeron**
IMP. SUBJ.   **(-se) leyese, leyeses,** *etc.*
IMP. SUBJ.   **(-ra) leyera, leyeras,** *etc.*
PRES. PART. **leyendo**
PAST PART.   leído

Other verbs of this type: **caer, creer, oír.**

10. Verbs in **-eír** (radical-changing). Note the written accents and the loss of one **i** in the third person preterit, imperfect subjunctive, and present participle.

reír (i), *to laugh*

PRES. IND.   **río, ríes, ríe, reímos, reís, ríen**
PRETERIT   reí, reíste, **rió,** reímos, reísteis, **rieron**
PRES. SUBJ.   **ría, rías, ría, riamos, riáis, rían**
IMP. SUBJ.   **(-se) riese, rieses,** *etc.*
IMP. SUBJ.   **(-ra) riera, rieras,** *etc.*
IMPERATIVE   **ríe,** reíd
PRES. PART.   **riendo**
PAST PART.   **reído**

Other verbs of this type: **freír,** *to fry;* **sonreír,** *to smile.*

11. Verbs in **-uir** (except **-guir** and **-quir**). Insert **y** (except before **i**) and change **i** to **y** between vowels.

incluir, *to enclose*

PRES. IND.   **incluyo, incluyes, incluye,** incluimos, incluís, **incluyen**
PRETERIT   incluí, incluiste, **incluyó,** incluimos, incluisteis, **incluyeron**
PRES. SUBJ.   **incluya, incluyas,** *etc.*
IMP. SUBJ.   **(-se) incluyese, incluyeses,** *etc.*
IMP. SUBJ.   **(-ra) incluyera, incluyeras,** *etc.*
IMPERATIVE   **incluye,** incluid
PRES. PART.   **incluyendo**

Other verbs of this type: **concluir,** *to end;* **construir,** *to construct.*

12. Verbs in **-iar.** Some **-iar** verbs have a stressed **i** with written accent on all forms (except first and second persons plural) of the present indicative and subjunctive, and on the imperative singular.

enviar, *to send*

PRES. IND.   **envío, envías, envía,** enviamos, enviáis, **envían**
PRES. SUBJ.   **envíe, envíes, envíe,** enviemos, enviéis, **envíen**
IMPERATIVE   **envía,** enviad

Other verbs of this type: **desviar,** *to divert;* **variar,** *to vary.*

13. Verbs in **-uar** (except **-guar**). Note the accented **u.**

continuar, *to continue*

PRES. IND.   **continúo, continúas, continúa,** continuamos, continuáis, **continúan**
PRES. SUBJ.   **continúe, continúes, continúe,** continuemos, continuéis, **continúen**
IMPERATIVE   **continúa,** continuad

Other verbs of this type: **acentuar,** *to accent;* **graduar,** *to graduate.*

14. **Verbs in -ll and ñ.** The i of the diphthongs **ie** and **io** is lost when the verb stem ends in **ll** or **ñ**.

bullir, *to boil*

PRETERIT   bullí, bulliste, bulló, bullimos, bullisteis, bulleron
IMP. SUBJ.   (-se) bullese, bulleses, *etc.*
IMP. SUBJ.   (-ra) bullera, bulleras, *etc.*
PRES. PART.   bullendo

reñir (i), *to scold, quarrel*

PRETERIT   reñí, reñiste, riñó, reñimos, reñisteis, riñeron
IMP. SUBJ.   (-se) riñese, riñeses, *etc.*
IMP. SUBJ.   (-ra) riñera, riñeras, *etc.*

Other verbs of this type: ceñir, *to gird;* gruñir, *to grunt, growl.*

133. Personal Pronouns

PERSON	SUBJECT	INDIRECT OBJECT	DIRECT OBJECT	REFLEX.	OBJECT OF A PREPOSITION
1	yo	me	me	me	(para) mí†
2	tú	te	te	te	(para) ti†
	usted		le, la		(para) usted
3	él	le (se)	le, lo	se	(para) él
	ella		la		(para) ella
1	nosotros -as	nos	nos	nos	(para) nosotros -as
2	vosotros -as	os	os	os	(para) vosotros -as
	ustedes				(para) ustedes
3	ellos -as	les (se)	los,* las	se	(para) ellos -as

* les is frequently found as direct object, masculine plural.
† With the preposition con, mí and ti become conmigo and contigo.

134. The Spanish Alphabet

LETTER	NAME	LETTER	NAME
a	a	n	ene
b	be	ñ	eñe
c	ce	o	o
ch	che	p	pe
d	de	q	cu
e	e	r	ere
f	efe	rr	erre
g	ge	s	ese
h	hache	t	te
i	i	u	u
j	jota	v	ve
l	ele	x	equis
ll	elle	y	y griega
m	eme	z	zeta

The names of all letters in Spanish are feminine (**la jota, la ese**). The letters **k** and **w** are found only in foreign words. In a Spanish vocabulary words beginning with **ch** follow those beginning with **c**; words beginning with **ll** follow those beginning with **l**, and **ñ** follows **n** (**señor** is placed after **sentir**). The letter **rr** is alphabetized as in English.

135. Table of Irregular Verbs

See pages 170–179.

136. Relative Pronouns

que, *who, whom, which, that,* is the commonest relative pronoun. It is used as subject or as object and refers to either persons or things. It is used after the prepositions **de, a, en, con,** to refer to things.

Juan es el muchacho que habla español.	*John is the boy who speaks Spanish.*
El libro que Vd. tiene es de María.	*The book that you have is Mary's.*

Es la casa en que vive mi hermano.	*It is the house in which my brother lives.*
La fuente de que hablamos está cerca.	*The spring of which we are speaking is near.*

quien (*pl.*, **quienes**), *who, whom,* refers only to persons. It is used (a) after prepositions, and (b) as a compound relative (i.e., a relative that contains its own antecedent).

(a) El señor con quien hablaba.	*The gentleman with whom I was speaking.*
El autor a quien escribo.	*The author to whom I am writing.*
(b) Quien estudia aprende.	*He who studies learns.*

el que (**la que, los que, las que**), *who, which,* is a combination of the demonstrative **el** and the relative **que.** It is used (a) as a compound relative; (b) as a simple relative after prepositions, especially those of more than one syllable; and (c) to avoid ambiguity when there is more than one possible antecedent. In cases (b) and (c) **el cual** may be used instead of **el que.**

(a) Los que tienen pan lo comen.	*Those who have bread eat it.*
(b) Me dió cuatro libros, entre los que (los cuales) había una obra de Galdós.	*He gave me four books, among which there was a work of Galdós.*
(c) Leo las obras de Pereda, las que (las cuales) me gustan mucho.	*I am reading the works of Pereda, which I like very much.*

The neuter form **lo que** (**lo cual**), *which,* is used when the antecedent is not a single word, but the whole preceding statement.

Ha perdido el dinero, lo que (lo cual) siento mucho.	*He has lost the money, which I regret very much.*

INFINITIVE	PARTICIPLES: PRESENT PAST	PRESENT INDICATIVE	PRESENT SUBJUNCTIVE	IMPERFECT INDICATIVE	FUTURE INDICATIVE
andar to walk, go	andando andado	ando andas anda andamos andáis andan	ande andes ande andemos andéis anden	andaba andabas andaba andábamos andabais andaban	andaré andarás andará andaremos andaréis andarán
asir to seize	asiendo asido	asgo ases ase asimos asís asen	asga asgas asga asgamos asgáis asgan	asía asías asía asíamos asíais asían	asiré asirás asirá asiremos asiréis asirán
caber to be contained in	cabiendo cabido	quepo cabes cabe cabemos cabéis caben	quepa quepas quepa quepamos quepáis quepan	cabía cabías cabía cabíamos cabíais cabían	cabré cabrás cabrá cabremos cabréis cabrán
caer to fall	cayendo caído	caigo caes cae caemos caéis caen	caiga caigas caiga caigamos caigáis caigan	caía caías caía caíamos caíais caían	caeré caerás caerá caeremos caeréis caerán
conducir to conduct (Similarly, all verbs in -ducir)	conduciendo conducido	conduzco conduces conduce conducimos conducís conducen	conduzca conduzcas conduzca conduzcamos conduzcáis conduzcan	conducía conducías conducía conducíamos conducíais conducían	conduciré conducirás conducirá conduciremos conduciréis conducirán
dar to give	dando dado	doy das da damos dais dan	dé des dé demos deis den	daba dabas daba dábamos dabais daban	daré darás dará daremos daréis darán

Conditional	Preterit Indicative	Imperfect Subjunctive	Imperfect Subjunctive	Imperative
andaría	anduve	anduviese	anduviera	
andarías	anduviste	anduvieses	anduvieras	anda
andaría	anduvo	anduviese	anduviera	
andaríamos	anduvimos	anduviésemos	anduviéramos	
andaríais	anduvisteis	anduvieseis	anduvierais	andad
andarían	anduvieron	anduviesen	anduvieran	
asiría	así	asiese	asiera	
asirías	asiste	asieses	asieras	ase
asiría	asió	asiese	asiera	
asiríamos	asimos	asiésemos	asiéramos	
asiríais	asisteis	asieseis	asierais	asid
asirían	asieron	asiesen	asieran	
cabría	cupe	cupiese	cupiera	
cabrías	cupiste	cupieses	cupieras	cabe
cabría	cupo	cupiese	cupiera	
cabríamos	cupimos	cupiésemos	cupiéramos	
cabríais	cupisteis	cupieseis	cupierais	cabed
cabrían	cupieron	cupiesen	cupieran	
caería	caí	cayese	cayera	
caerías	caíste	cayeses	cayeras	cae
caería	cayó	cayese	cayera	
caeríamos	caímos	cayésemos	cayéramos	
caeríais	caísteis	cayeseis	cayerais	caed
caerían	cayeron	cayesen	cayeran	
conduciría	conduje	condujese	condujera	
conducirías	condujiste	condujeses	condujeras	conduce
conduciría	condujo	condujese	condujera	
conduciríamos	condujimos	condujésemos	condujéramos	
conduciríais	condujisteis	condujeseis	condujerais	conducid
conducirían	condujeron	condujesen	condujeran	
daría	di	diese	diera	
darías	diste	dieses	dieras	da
daría	dió	diese	diera	
daríamos	dimos	diésemos	diéramos	
daríais	disteis	dieseis	dierais	dad
darían	dieron	diesen	dieran	

Infinitive	Participles: Present Past	Present Indicative	Present Subjunctive	Imperfect Indicative	Future Indicative
decir *to say, tell*	diciendo	digo	diga	decía	diré
		dices	digas	decías	dirás
		dice	diga	decía	dirá
	dicho	decimos	digamos	decíamos	diremos
		decís	digáis	decíais	diréis
		dicen	digan	decían	dirán
errar *to err*	errando	yerro	yerre	erraba	erraré
		yerras	yerres	errabas	errarás
		yerra	yerre	erraba	errará
	errado	erramos	erremos	errábamos	erraremos
		erráis	erréis	errabais	erraréis
		yerran	yerren	erraban	errarán
estar *to be*	estando	estoy	esté	estaba	estaré
		estás	estés	estabas	estarás
		está	esté	estaba	estará
	estado	estamos	estemos	estábamos	estaremos
		estáis	estéis	estabais	estaréis
		están	estén	estaban	estarán
haber *to have*	habiendo	he	haya	había	habré
		has	hayas	habías	habrás
		ha	haya	había	habrá
	habido	hemos	hayamos	habíamos	habremos
		habéis	hayáis	habíais	habréis
		han	hayan	habían	habrán
hacer *to do, make*	haciendo	hago	haga	hacía	haré
		haces	hagas	hacías	harás
		hace	haga	hacía	hará
	hecho	hacemos	hagamos	hacíamos	haremos
		hacéis	hagáis	hacíais	haréis
		hacen	hagan	hacían	harán
ir *to go*	yendo	voy	vaya	iba	iré
		vas	vayas	ibas	irás
		va	vaya	iba	irá
	ido	vamos	vayamos	íbamos	iremos
		vais	vayáis	ibais	iréis
		van	vayan	iban	irán

Conditional	Preterit Indicative	Imperfect Subjunctive	Imperfect Subjunctive	Imperative
diría	dije	dijese	dijera	
dirías	dijiste	dijeses	dijeras	di
diría	dijo	dijese	dijera	
diríamos	dijimos	dijésemos	dijéramos	
diríais	dijisteis	dijeseis	dijerais	decid
dirían	dijeron	dijesen	dijeran	
erraría	erré	errase	errara	
errarías	erraste	errases	erraras	yerra
erraría	erró	errase	errara	
erraríamos	erramos	errásemos	erráramos	
erraríais	errasteis	erraseis	errarais	errad
errarían	erraron	errasen	erraran	
estaría	estuve	estuviese	estuviera	
estarías	estuviste	estuvieses	estuvieras	está
estaría	estuvo	estuviese	estuviera	
estaríamos	estuvimos	estuviésemos	estuviéramos	
estaríais	estuvisteis	estuvieseis	estuvierais	estad
estarían	estuvieron	estuviesen	estuvieran	
habría	hube	hubiese	hubiera	
habrías	hubiste	hubieses	hubieras	(he)
habría	hubo	hubiese	hubiera	
habríamos	hubimos	hubiésemos	hubiéramos	
habríais	hubisteis	hubieseis	hubierais	habed
habrían	hubieron	hubiesen	hubieran	
haría	hice	hiciese	hiciera	
harías	hiciste	hicieses	hicieras	haz
haría	hizo	hiciese	hiciera	
haríamos	hicimos	hiciésemos	hiciéramos	
haríais	hicisteis	hicieseis	hicierais	haced
harían	hicieron	hiciesen	hicieran	
iría	fuí	fuese	fuera	
irías	fuiste	fueses	fueras	ve
iría	fué	fuese	fuera	
iríamos	fuimos	fuésemos	fuéramos	
iríais	fuisteis	fueseis	fuerais	id
irían	fueron	fuesen	fueran	

Infinitive	Participles: Present Past	Present Indicative	Present Subjunctive	Imperfect Indicative	Future Indicative
jugar *to play* *(a game)*	jugando jugado	juego juegas juega jugamos jugáis juegan	juegue juegues juegue juguemos juguéis jueguen	jugaba jugabas jugaba jugábamos jugabais jugaban	jugaré jugarás jugará jugaremos jugaréis jugarán
oír *to hear*	oyendo oído	oigo oyes oye oímos oís oyen	oiga oigas oiga oigamos oigáis oigan	oía oías oía oíamos oíais oían	oiré oirás oirá oiremos oiréis oirán
oler *to smell*	oliendo olido	huelo hueles huele olemos oléis huelen	huela huelas huela olamos oláis huelan	olía olías olía olíamos olíais olían	oleré olerás olerá oleremos oleréis olerán
poder *to be able*	pudiendo podido	puedo puedes puede podemos podéis pueden	pueda puedas pueda podamos podáis puedan	podía podías podía podíamos podíais podían	podré podrás podrá podremos podréis podrán
poner *to put, place*	poniendo puesto	pongo pones pone ponemos ponéis ponen	ponga pongas ponga pongamos pongáis pongan	ponía ponías ponía poníamos poníais ponían	pondré pondrás pondrá pondremos pondréis pondrán
querer *to wish, will*	queriendo querido	quiero quieres quiere queremos queréis quieren	quiera quieras quiera queramos queráis quieran	quería querías quería queríamos queríais querían	querré querrás querrá querremos querréis querrán

Conditional	Preterit Indicative	Imperfect Subjunctive	Imperfect Subjunctive	Imperative
jugaría	jugué	jugase	jugara	
jugarías	jugaste	jugases	jugaras	juega
jugaría	jugó	jugase	jugara	
jugaríamos	jugamos	jugásemos	jugáramos	
jugaríais	jugasteis	jugaseis	jugarais	jugad
jugarían	jugaron	jugasen	jugaran	
oiría	oí	oyese	oyera	
oirías	oíste	oyeses	oyeras	oye
oiría	oyó	oyese	oyera	
oiríamos	oímos	oyésemos	oyéramos	
oiríais	oísteis	oyeseis	oyerais	oíd
oirían	oyeron	oyesen	oyeran	
olería	olí	oliese	oliera	
olerías	oliste	olieses	olieras	huele
olería	olió	oliese	oliera	
oleríamos	olimos	oliésemos	oliéramos	
oleríais	olisteis	olieseis	olierais	oled
olerían	olieron	oliesen	olieran	
podría	pude	pudiese	pudiera	
podrías	pudiste	pudieses	pudieras	
podría	pudo	pudiese	pudiera	
podríamos	pudimos	pudiésemos	pudiéramos	
podríais	pudisteis	pudieseis	pudierais	
podrían	pudieron	pudiesen	pudieran	
pondría	puse	pusiese	pusiera	
pondrías	pusiste	pusieses	pusieras	pon
pondría	puso	pusiese	pusiera	
pondríamos	pusimos	pusiésemos	pusiéramos	
pondríais	pusisteis	pusieseis	pusierais	poned
pondrían	pusieron	pusiesen	pusieran	
querría	quise	quisiese	quisiera	
querrías	quisiste	quisieses	quisieras	quiere
querría	quiso	quisiese	quisiera	
querríamos	quisimos	quisiésemos	quisiéramos	
querríais	quisisteis	quisieseis	quisierais	quered
querrían	quisieron	quisiesen	quisieran	

Infinitive	Participles: Present Past	Present Indicative	Present Subjunctive	Imperfect Indicative	Future Indicative
saber *to know,* *know how*	sabiendo sabido	sé sabes sabe sabemos sabéis saben	sepa sepas sepa sepamos sepáis sepan	sabía sabías sabía sabíamos sabíais sabían	sabré sabrás sabrá sabremos sabréis sabrán
salir *to go out,* *leave*	saliendo salido	salgo sales sale salimos salís salen	salga salgas salga salgamos salgáis salgan	salía salías salía salíamos salíais salían	saldré saldrás saldrá saldremos saldréis saldrán
ser *to be*	siendo sido	soy eres es somos sois son	sea seas sea seamos seáis sean	era eras era éramos erais eran	seré serás será seremos seréis serán
tener *to have*	teniendo tenido	tengo tienes tiene tenemos tenéis tienen	tenga tengas tenga tengamos tengáis tengan	tenía tenías tenía teníamos teníais tenían	tendré tendrás tendrá tendremos tendréis tendrán
traer *to bring*	trayendo traído	traigo traes trae traemos traéis traen	traiga traigas traiga traigamos traigáis traigan	traía traías traía traíamos traíais traían	traeré traerás traerá traeremos traeréis traerán
valer *to be* *worth*	valiendo valido	valgo vales vale valemos valéis valen	valga valgas valga valgamos valgáis valgan	valía valías valía valíamos valíais valían	valdré valdrás valdrá valdremos valdréis valdrán

Conditional	Preterit Indicative	Imperfect Subjunctive	Imperfect Subjunctive	Imperative
sabría	supe	supiese	supiera	
sabrías	supiste	supieses	supieras	sabe
sabría	supo	supiese	supiera	
sabríamos	supimos	supiésemos	supiéramos	
sabríais	supisteis	supieseis	supierais	sabed
sabrían	supieron	supiesen	supieran	
saldría	salí	saliese	saliera	
saldrías	saliste	salieses	salieras	sal
saldría	salió	saliese	saliera	
saldríamos	salimos	saliésemos	saliéramos	
saldríais	salisteis	salieseis	salierais	salid
saldrían	salieron	saliesen	salieran	
sería	fuí	ruese	fuera	
serías	fuiste	fueses	fueras	sé
sería	fué	fuese	fuera	
seríamos	fuimos	fuésemos	fuéramos	
seríais	fuisteis	fueseis	fuerais	sed
serían	fueron	fuesen	fueran	
tendría	tuve	tuviese	tuviera	
tendrías	tuviste	tuvieses	tuvieras	ten
tendría	tuvo	tuviese	tuviera	
tendríamos	tuvimos	tuviésemos	tuviéramos	
tendríais	tuvisteis	tuvieseis	tuvierais	tened
tendrían	tuvieron	tuviesen	tuvieran	
traería	traje	trajese	trajera	
traerías	trajiste	trajeses	trajeras	trae
traería	trajo	trajese	trajera	
traeríamos	trajimos	trajésemos	trajéramos	
traeríais	trajisteis	trajeseis	trajerais	traed
traerían	trajeron	trajesen	trajeran	
valdría	valí	valiese	valiera	
valdrías	valiste	valieses	valieras	val(e)
valdría	valió	valiese	valiera	
valdríamos	valimos	valiésemos	valiéramos	
valdríais	valisteis	valieseis	valierais	valed
valdrían	valieron	valiesen	valieran	

INFINITIVE	PARTICIPLES: PRESENT PAST	PRESENT INDICATIVE	PRESENT SUBJUNCTIVE	IMPERFECT INDICATIVE	FUTURE INDICATIVE
venir *to come*	viniendo venido	vengo vienes viene venimos venís vienen	venga vengas venga vengamos vengáis vengan	venía venías venía veníamos veníais venían	vendré vendrás vendrá vendremos vendréis vendrán
ver *to see*	viendo visto	veo ves ve vemos veis ven	vea vcas vea veamos veáis vean	veía veías veía veíamos veíais veían	veré verás verá veremos veréis verán

Conditional	Preterit Indicative	Imperfect Subjunctive	Imperfect Subjunctive	Imperative
vendría	vine	viniese	viniera	
vendrías	viniste	vinieses	vinieras	ven
vendría	vino	viniese	viniera	
vendríamos	vinimos	viniésemos	viniéramos	
vendríais	vinisteis	vinieseis	vinierais	venid
vendrían	vinieron	viniesen	vinieran	
vería	vi	viese	viera	
verías	viste	vieses	vieras	ve
vería	vió	viese	viera	
veríamos	vimos	viésemos	viéramos	
veríais	visteis	vieseis	vierais	ved
verían	vieron	viesen	vieran	

Spanish-English Vocabulary [1]

A

a, to, at

abajo, down, below; downstairs; **ir calle —,** to go down the street

abierto, opened, open

abril, April

abrir, to open

la abuela, grandmother

el abuelo, grandfather

acá, here, hither

acabar, to finish; (*with* **de** *and inf.*), to have just . . .; **acaba de** (**entrar**), he has just (entered); **acababa de** (**entrar**), he had just (entered)

la acción, action

acercarse (a), to approach

acompañar, to accompany

acostar (ue), to put to bed; **—se,** to go to bed

el acto, act

además, besides

adiós, good-by

¿adónde? where (*to what place*)?

advertir (ie), to warn

agosto, August

el agua *f.*, water

ahí, there (*near by*)

ahora, now

el aire, air

alcanzar, to overtake, reach

alegrarse (de), to rejoice, be glad

alegre, merry

alemán, German

algo, something

alguien, someone, somebody

alguno, some; *pl.*, some, a few

el alma *f.*, soul

alto, tall, high; **en voz —a,** in a loud voice

allá, there; **más —,** beyond; farther on

allí, there, over there

amar, to love

ambos *adj. and pro.*, both

el amigo, friend

el amo, master, employer

el amor, love

Ana, Anna

andar, to go, run (*of a machine*); to walk

el animal, animal

anoche, last night

ante, before (*place*)

antes, before, formerly; *prep.*, **— de,** before (*time*)

antiguo, old

Antonio, Anthony

añadir, to add

el año, year; **¿cuántos —s tiene (su tío)?** how old is (your uncle)? **cumplir (diez) —s,** to reach

---

one's (tenth) birthday; **tener** (**cinco**) —s, to be (five) years old

aparecer, to appear

apartar, to push aside *or* away

aparte, aside

apenas, hardly, scarcely

aprender, to learn

aquel (**aquella, aquellos, aquellas**), that (*yonder*)

aquél *pro.*, that, that one

aquello, that (*neut. pro.*)

aquí, here; — **lo tiene Vd.**, here it is

el **árbol**, tree

arriba, above, up; upstairs; **ir calle** —, to go up the street

el **arte** (*m. & f.*), art

así, so, thus

atreverse (**a**), to dare

aun (*when emphatic, after the verb,* **aún**), still, yet; even

aunque, although, even if

el **automóvil**, automobile

el **autor**, author

ayer, yesterday

ayudar, to help

B

bajar, to go down, come down; to lower

bajo, low, short

bastante, enough; — **bien**, rather well

bastar, to be enough

beber, to drink

bello, beautiful

bien, well; *noun*, good

blanco, white

la **boca**, mouth

bonito, pretty

el **brazo**, arm; **coge del** — **a** (**su amigo**), he seizes (his friend) by the arm

bueno, good; *with* **estar**, well

buscar, to look for

C

el **caballero**, knight, gentleman

el **caballo**, horse; **a** —, on horseback

la **cabeza**, head; **dolor de** —, headache

cada, each, every

caer, to fall

el **café**, coffee; café

caliente, warm, hot

el **calor**, heat; **hace** (**mucho**) —, it is (very) warm

callar, to be silent; to keep quiet

la **calle**, street

el **cambio**, change; **en** —, on the other hand

el **camino**, road

el **campo**, country, field

cansado, tired

cantar, to sing

la **cara**, face

Carlos, Charles

la **carne**, meat

la **carta**, letter

la **casa**, house; **a** — **de** (**mi tío**), to (my uncle's); **en** —, at home, in the house; **en** — **de** (**mi tío**), at (my uncle's); **ir a** —, to go home

casarse (**con**), to marry, get married

casi, almost, nearly

el **caso**, case

la **causa**, cause

cerca (**de**), near

cerrar (ie), to close

el cielo, heaven; sky

la ciencia, science

cierto, certain

la ciudad, city

claro, clear

la clase, class; classroom; kind; ¿qué — de . . . ? what kind of . . . ?

el coche, car, cab

coger, to seize, catch; coge del brazo a (su amigo), he seizes (his friend) by the arm

colocar, to place; —se, to get a job (place oneself)

el color, color

comenzar (ie), to commence, begin

comer, to eat

como, as, since, like

¿cómo? how? ¿ — se llama? what is his name?

el compañero, companion

la compañía, company

completo, complete; por —, completely

comprar, to buy

comprender, to understand

con, with

la condición, condition

conducir, to lead, conduct; to drive (a car)

conmigo, with me

conocer, to know (be acquainted with); to meet

conservar, to preserve, keep

considerar, to consider; bien considerado, on second thought

contar (ue), to count; to tell, relate

la contestación, answer

contestar, to answer

contigo fam., with you

contra, against

contrario, contrary; al —, on the contrary

el corazón, heart

correr, to run

cortar, to cut

corto, short

la cosa, thing; otra —, something (anything) else

la costumbre, custom, habit

creer, to believe, think

el criado, servant; la criada, servant girl, maid

el cristal, glass

el cuadro, picture

¿cuál? pl., ¿cuáles? what? which?

cualquier(a), any; cualquiera pro., anyone

cuando, when; de vez en —, from time to time

cuanto, all (that), as much as; en cuanto, as soon as; en cuanto a, as for, concerning

¿cuánto? how much? pl., how many?

el cuarto, room

cubierto, covered

cubrir, to cover

la cuenta, bill; darse — de, to realize

el cuento, story

el cuerpo, body

el cuidado, care; con —, carefully

cumplir, to fulfill; — (diez) años, to reach one's (tenth) birthday, — palabra, to keep (one's) word

cuyo, whose, of which

CH

el **chico**, small boy, youngster

D

dar, to give; to strike; —se cuenta de, to realize

de, of, from, with

debajo de, under

deber, to owe, ought to (should)

decir, to say, tell; — que sí (que no), to say yes (no); quiero —, I mean

el **dedo**, finger, toe

la **defensa**, defense

dejar, to leave; to allow; — de (+ *inf.*), to stop; to fail; no deje Vd. de hacerlo, do not fail to do it

delante de, in front of

demás: los —, the others, the rest

dentro, inside; — de, within

derecho, right; a la —a, to (at) the right

descubrir, to discover

desde, from, since

desear, to desire

el **deseo**, desire

desesperar, to despair

despedirse (i) de, to say good-by to; to take leave of

despertar (ie), to awaken; —se, to wake up

después, afterward, then; — de, after

detener, to detain, stop; —se, to stop (*intransitive*)

detrás de, behind

el **día**, the day; al — siguiente, on the following day; buenos —s, good morning; (dos pesos) al —,

(two dollars) a (per) day; todos los —s, every day; (tres veces) al —, (three times) a day

diciembre, December

el **diente**, tooth

difícil, difficult

digno, worthy

el **dinero**, money

Dios, God

dirigir, to direct; —se a, to make one's way toward

disponer, to arrange, prepare; —se, to get ready

distinguir, to distinguish

el **dolor**, pain; — de cabeza, headache

el **domingo**, Sunday

don (doña), *title equivalent to Mr. (Mrs.), but used only before the first name; not translated*

¿dónde? where?

donde *rel.*, where

dormir (ue), to sleep

la **duda**, doubt

dudar, to doubt

el **dueño**, owner, proprietor

dulce, sweet

durante, during

duro, hard; pan —, stale bread; *noun* dollar

E

e, and (*before a word beginning with* i *or* hi)

echar, to throw; — a (la calle), to throw into (the street); — a (correr), to start to (run)

la **edad**, age

el **efecto**, effect; en —, in fact, as a matter of fact

el ejemplo, example
el, the
el embargo: sin —, nevertheless
empezar (ie), to begin
emplear, to employ, use
en, in, on
encontrar (ue), to meet; to find
el enemigo, enemy
enero, January
enfermo, ill, sick
engañar, to deceive
enseñar, to show; to teach
entender (ie), to understand
entero, entire, whole
entonces, then; pues —, well
then
entrar (en), to enter, go in, come
in; — en relaciones con, to enter
into (establish) business connections with
entre, between, among
entregar, to deliver, hand (over)
enviar, to send
la escena, scene; stage
escribir, to write
escuchar, to listen (to)
la escuela, school; a la —, to school
ese (esa, esos, esas), that (near
by)
ése pro., that, that one
eso neut. pro., that; por eso, therefore, for that reason
el espacio, space, room
España, Spain
español, Spanish; noun, Spanish,
Spaniard
la esperanza, hope
esperar, to hope, expect; to wait
for
el espíritu, spirit

el esposo, husband; la esposa, wife
el estado, state, condition
estar, to be (in a place, state, or
condition)
este (esta, estos, estas), this
éste pro., this, this one
el estudio, study
eterno, eternal, everlasting
Europa, Europe
existir, to exist

F

fácil, easy
fácilmente, easily
la falta, lack, need; hacen — (tales
locos), (such madmen) are
needed; me hace — (dinero), I
need (money)
faltar, to lack, be lacking
la familia, family
el favor, favor; hágame el — de
(decírmelo), please (tell me)
la fe, faith
febrero, February
feliz, happy (used with ser)
feo, ugly, homely
la figura, figure
figurarse, to imagine
el fin, end; al —, at last; en —, in
short
la flor, flower
el fondo, bottom
la forma, form
formar, to form
la fortuna, fortune
francés, French; noun, French,
Frenchman
la frente, forehead
fresco -a, fresh, cool; agua —a,
cold water

el frío, cold; hace —, it is cold
el fuego, fire
la fuente, fountain; spring
  fuera de, outside of, aside from
  fuerte, strong
la fuerza, force; strength; *pl.*,
  strength

G

ganar, to gain, earn
general, general (*adj. & noun*)
la gente, people
la gloria, glory
  gozar (de), to enjoy
la gracia, grace; *pl.*, thanks
  grande, large, big
  grave, grave, serious
  guardar, to guard, keep, save
la guerra, war
  gustar, to be pleasing to; to like
el gusto, taste; pleasure; con mucho
  —, gladly

H

la Habana, Havana
  haber, to have (*auxiliary*)
la habitación, room, bedroom
  hablar, to speak, talk
  hacer, to do, make; hace (mucho)
  calor, it is (very) warm; hacen
  falta (tales locos), (such madmen) are needed; hace (un
  mes), (a month) ago; hágame
  el favor de (decírmelo), please
  (tell me); me hace falta (dinero), I need (money)
  hacia, toward
  hallar, to find
el hambre *f.*, hunger; tener —, to be
  hungry

hasta, until; — que, until; —
  luego, good-by, so long
hay, there is, there are; — sol, the
  sun is shining
la hermana, sister
el hermano, brother
  hermoso, beautiful
el hijo, son; *pl.*, children
la historia, history; story
el hombre, man
el honor, honor
la hora, hour, time (*of day*)
  hoy, today
  huir, to flee
  humano, human

I

la idea, idea
la iglesia, church; a la —, to church
  igual, equal, same; like; alike
  importar, to matter; to be important
  imposible, impossible
  indicar, to indicate
la industria, industry
  inglés, English; *noun*, Englishman
el instante, instant
  interesante, interesting
el invierno, winter
  ir, to go; — a casa, to go home;
  —se, to go away
la isla, island
  italiano, Italian
  izquierdo, left

J

jamás, never, ever
el jardín, (flower) garden
José, Joseph

joven, young; *noun*, young man, young woman

Juan, John

el jueves, Thursday

julio, July

junio, June

junto a, by, beside

la justicia, justice

L

la, the

el labio, lip; — superior (inferior), upper (lower) lip

el lado, side; al — de, beside

el ladrón, thief

la lágrima, tear; tiene los ojos llenos de —s, her eyes are full of tears

el lápiz, pencil

largo, long

leer, to read

lejos, far, far away

la lengua, tongue, language

lento, slow

la letra, letter (*of the alphabet*); handwriting

letrado, learned

levantar, to raise, lift; —se, to rise, get up

la ley, law

la libertad, liberty

libre, free

el libro, book; — de memorias, memorandum book

la linterna, lantern

loco, mad, crazy; *noun*, madman; volverse —, to become (go) crazy

luego, then, afterward; hasta —, good-by, so long

el lugar, place, village

Luis, Louis

el lunes, Monday

la luz, light

LL

llamar, to call; — (a la puerta), to knock (at the door); —se, to be called; to be named; ¿cómo se llama? what is his name? se llama (Juan), his name is (John)

llegar, to arrive; — a, to arrive in; — a ser, to get to be, become

llenar, to fill

lleno, full; tiene los ojos —s de lágrimas, her eyes are full of tears

llevar, to take, carry; wear (*of clothes*)

llorar, to weep, mourn

llover (ue), to rain

la lluvia, rain

M

la madre, mother

el maestro, teacher

el mal, evil, harm

mal, badly

malo, bad; (*with estar*), ill, sick

mandar, to command, order; to send

la manera, manner, way; de — que, so that

la mano, hand

la mañana, morning; *adv.*, tomorrow

la mar, sea

María, Mary

el marido, husband

el martes, Tuesday

marzo, March

más, more; *adv.,* more; **— allá,** beyond, farther on

matar, to kill

mayo, May

mayor, larger, largest; **la — parte de,** most of

el mazo, mallet, wooden hammer

medio, half

mejor, better, best

la memoria, memory; *pl.,* memoranda; **libro de —s,** memorandum book

menor, smaller, smallest

menos, less; except; **por lo —,** at least

la mentira, falsehood, lie

merecer, to merit, deserve

el mes, month

la mesa, table; desk

meter, to put in; **—se en (el agua),** to plunge into (the water)

el miedo, fear; **tener —,** to be afraid

mientras, while

el miércoles, Wednesday

Miguel, Michael

el minuto, minute

mirar, to look (at)

mismo, same; myself, yourself, himself, *etc.*

el modo, way, manner; **de — que,** so, so that; **de (este) —,** in (this) way; **de otro —,** otherwise

el momento, moment

la mona, monkey

la montaña, mountain

morir (ue), to die

la mosca, fly

mostrar (ue), to show

mover (ue), to move; **—se,** to move (*intransitive*)

el movimiento, movement

la muchacha, girl

el muchacho, boy

mucho, much; *pl.,* many

la muerte, death

la mujer, woman, wife

el mundo, world; **todo el —,** everybody

muy, very

N

nacer, to be born

nada, nothing, anything; **de —,** you are welcome, don't mention it

nadie, no one, nobody, anybody

la nariz, nose

natural, natural

la naturaleza, nature

naturalmente, naturally, of course

necesario, necessary

la necesidad, necessity, need

necesitar, to need

negar (ie), to deny; **—se a,** to refuse

negro, black

ni, nor; **ni . . . ni,** neither . . . nor

ninguno, no, not one; any; *pro.,* nobody, anybody

el niño, child, little boy; *f.,* child, little girl; *pl.,* children

no, no, not

noble, noble

la noche, night; **esta —,** tonight; **por la —,** at night

el nombre, name

noviembre, November

nuevo, new

el número, number

nunca, never

O

o, or; o . . . o, either . . . or
el objeto, object
obligar (a), to oblige, compel
la obra, work
obscuro, dark
la ocasión, occasion
octubre, October
ocupar, to occupy
ofrecer, to offer
oír, to hear; to listen
el ojo, eye; tiene los —s llenos de lágrimas, her eyes are full of tears
olvidar, to forget
la orden, order
la oreja, ear
el orgullo, pride
el oro, gold
el otoño, autumn
otro, other, another; —a vez, again

P

Paco, Frank
el padre, father; *pl.*, parents
pagar, to pay; to pay for
el país, country
la palabra, word; cumplir —, to fulfill a promise, keep (one's) word
el palacio, palace
el pan, bread; — duro, stale bread
el papel, paper
para, for, in order to; to
parecer, to appear, seem; to think
la pared, wall
la parte, part; la mayor — de, most of
partir, to depart

pasar, to pass; to happen; to spend (*time*); ¿qué te pasa? what's the matter with you?
el paso, step, pace
la paz, peace
el pecho, breast
el pedazo, piece
pedir (i), to ask for; to order
el pelo, hair
la pena, grief, distress
el pensamiento, thought
pensar (ie), to think; to intend, — en, to think about
peor, worse, worst
Pepe, Joe
pequeño, small, little
perder (ie), to lose; to waste
permitir, to permit
pero, but
la persona, person
pesar, to weigh
el pesar: a — de, in spite of
el pescado, fish
el peso, weight; dollar
el pie, foot; a —, on foot
la piedra, stone
la pierna, leg
el placer, pleasure
el plato, plate, dish
la pluma, pen
pobre, poor
la pobreza, poverty
poco, little; *pl.*, few
poder (ue), to be able, can
el poeta, poet
poner, to put, place; —se, to put on; —se a (trabajar), to begin (to work); —se (malo), to become (ill)
por, for, by, through, along; — el

camino, along the road; — eso, therefore, for that reason

¿por qué? why?

porque, because

portugués, Portuguese

posible, possible

preciso, necessary

la pregunta, question; hacer una —, to ask a question

preguntar, to ask, inquire

presentar, to present; to introduce

presente, present

la prima, cousin (f.); el primo, cousin (m.)

la primavera, spring

la princesa, princess

principal, principal, main

el príncipe, prince

el principio, beginning; al —, at first

la prisa, haste, hurry; tener —, to be in a hurry

procurar, to try

producir, to produce

profundo, profound, deep

pronto, quickly, soon; de —, suddenly

propio, one's own; private

el propósito, purpose; a —, by the way

el público, public

el pueblo, town, village; people

la puerta, door; llamar a la —, to knock at the door

pues, well, since; — entonces, well then

el puesto, place

el punto, point

puro, pure

Q

que rel. pro., who, which, that; conj., that

¿qué? what?

¡qué! what a!

quedar(se), to remain, stay; me quedan (dos pesos), I have (two dollars) left (two dollars remain to me); me quedo en casa, I stay home

querer, to will; to wish, want; quiere a (María), he loves (Mary); quiero decir, I mean

querido, dear

quien, who, whom

¿quién? pl., ¿quiénes? who? whom?

quitar, to remove; —se, to take off

quizá(s), perhaps

R

rápidamente, rapidly

rápido, rapid, quick

el rato, short space of time, while; al poco —, in a little while

la razón, reason; no tener —, to be wrong; tener —, to be right

real, royal, real

recibir, to receive

recoger, to pick up

recordar (ue), to remember

el recuerdo, remembrance; pl., regards

referir (ie), to refer; —se a, to refer to

la reina, queen

reír, to laugh; —se de, to laugh at

la relación, relation; *pl.*, (business) relations, connections; entrar en —es con, to enter into (establish) business connections with

relucir, to shine, glitter

repetir (i), to repeat

el respecto, relation (*used only in prepositional phrases*); — a, with regard to

el respeto, respect

responder, to reply, answer

la respuesta, answer

reunirse, to meet; to get together

el rey, king

rico, rich

el río, river

la riqueza, wealth

rogar (ue), to pray, beg, ask

romper, to break, tear

la rosa, rose

el rostro, face

roto, broken, torn

el ruido, noise

S

el sábado, Saturday

saber, to know; to know how (can)

sacar, to take out; to get out

la sal, salt

salir (de), to leave, go out

la salud, health

la sangre, blood

sano, sound, healthy

el santo (la santa), saint

el secreto, secret

la sed, thirst; tener —, to be thirsty

la seda, silk

la seguida: en —, at once, immediately

seguir (i), to follow; to continue

según, according to, as

seguro, sure

la semana, week

semejante, similar, alike

sentado, seated

sentar (ie), to seat; —se, to sit down

el sentido, sense

el sentimiento, sentiment, feeling

sentir (ie), to feel; to be sorry, regret

el señor, gentleman; Mr., sir

la señora, madam, Mrs.; lady; la — de (Morales), Mrs. (Morales)

la señorita, Miss, young lady

el señorito, young gentleman, Mr. (*used by servants*)

septiembre, September

ser, to be; es verdad, it is true; ¿no es verdad? isn't it so? doesn't he? *etc.;* llegar a —, to get to be, to become

servir (i), to serve

severo, severe

si, if; whether

sí, yes; decir que —, to say yes

sí (*reflex. obj. of a prep.*), himself, herself, itself, themselves

siempre, always

el siglo, century

siguiente, following; al día —, on the following day

sin, without

sino, but

el sitio, place

sobre, on, upon; — todo, especially

el sol, sun; hay —, the sun is shining

soler (ue), to be accustomed

solo, alone

sólo, only

la sombra, shade; a la — de, in the shade of

el sombrero, hat

su, your, his, her, their

subir, to go up; — a (un árbol), to climb (a tree)

suceder, to happen

el suelo, floor, ground

el sueño, sleep; en —s, in (one's) dreams

la suerte, luck

sufrir, to suffer

suponer, to suppose; por supuesto, of course

T

tal, such; such a; — vez, perhaps

también, also, too

tampoco, neither, either

tan, so, as

tanto, so, so much; as much; pl., so many, as many

la tarde, afternoon; adv., late; por la —, in the afternoon

el teatro, theater

temer, to fear

temprano, early

tener, to have (possess); — (cinco) años, to be (five) years old; — que (escribir), to have to (write); — razón, to be right; no — razón, to be wrong; aquí lo tiene Vd., here it is; ¿cuántos años tiene (su tío)? how old is (your uncle)? tiene los ojos llenos de lágrimas, her eyes are full of tears

terminar, to finish, end

el término, end; term, word

el tiempo, time; weather

la tierra, earth, land; (native) country

la tinta, ink

el tío, uncle; la tía, aunt

tocar, to touch; to concern; to play (a musical instrument)

todavía, yet, still; — no, not yet

todo, all, whole, every; — el mundo, everybody; —s los días, every day; sobre —, especially

tomar, to take

trabajar, to work

el trabajo, work

traer, to bring

traidor, deceitful, treacherous

el traje, suit

tratar, to treat; to try

el trecho, space, distance

triste, sad

tristemente, sadly

U

u, or (before a word beginning with o or ho)

último, last

un, a, an; one

una, a, an, one

único, only, unique

unir, to join; unite; —se, to unite

unos, some

usar, to use

usted, you

V

valer, to be worth

el valor, value, worth

vario, different; pl., several

el vecino, neighbor

vender, to sell

venir, to come

la ventana, window
ver, to see
el verano, summer
la verdad, truth; es —, it is true;
    ¿no es — ? *or* ¿ — ? isn't it so?
    doesn't he? *etc.*
verdadero, true, real
verde, green
el vestido, dress
vestir (i), to dress
la vez (*pl.*, veces), time; a veces, at
    times; algunas veces, some-
    times; de — en cuando, from
    time to time; en — de, instead
    of; muchas veces, often; otra —,
    again; por primera —, for the
    first time; tal —, perhaps
el viaje, trip, voyage
la vida, life
viejo, old; *noun*, old man; —a, old
    woman
el viento, wind; hace —, it is windy

el viernes, Friday
el vino, wine
la virtud, virtue
la vista, view
vivir, to live
vivo, alive; lively; bright
la voluntad, will
volver (ue), to return; —se loco,
    to become (go) crazy; vuelve a
    (leerlo), (he reads it) again
la voz, voice; en — alta, in a loud
    voice

Y

y, and
ya, now, already; — no, no longer
yerra, *3d per. sing. pres. of* errar
    (ie), to err

Z

el zapato, shoe

English-Spanish Vocabulary

A

a, un, una
able: to be —, poder (ue)
above, arriba
accompany, acompañar
according to, según
accustomed: to be —, soler (ue)
act, el acto
action, la acción
add, añadir
afraid: to be —, tener miedo
after, después de
afternoon, la tarde; in the —, por la tarde
afterward, después, luego
again, otra vez; volver a (+ *inf.*)
against, contra
age, la edad
ago: (two days) —, hace (dos días)
air, el aire
alike, igual, semejante
alive, vivo
all, todo
allow, dejar, permitir
almost, casi
alone, solo
along, por; — the road, por el camino
already, ya
also, también
although, aunque
always, siempre
among, entre

and, y; e (*before* i *or* hi)
animal, el animal
another, otro
answer, contestar, responder; la con· testación, la respuesta
any, algun(o), ningun(o); cualquier(a)
anyone, alguien, alguno; nadie, cualquiera
appear, aparecer, parecer
approach, acercarse (a)
April, abril
arm, el brazo
arrive, llegar; to — in, llegar a
art, arte (*m. & f.*)
as, como; tan; según; — soon —, en cuanto
aside, aparte; — from, fuera de
ask, preguntar; — for, pedir (i)
at, a
August, agosto
aunt, la tía; uncle and —, los tíos
author, el autor
automobile, el automóvil
autumn, el otoño
awaken, despertar (ie), wake up, despertarse

B

bad, malo
badly, mal
be, ser, estar
beautiful, hermoso, bello
because, porque

before, (*time*) antes (de); (*place*) ante, delante de

beg, rogar (ue)

begin, empezar (ie); to — (to work), ponerse a (trabajar)

beginning, el principio

behind, detrás de

believe, creer

besides, además

between, entre

beyond, más allá

big, grande

bill, la cuenta

black, negro

blood, la sangre

body, el cuerpo

book, el libro; memorandum —, libro de memorias

born: to be —, nacer

both, ambos; los dos

bottom, el fondo

boy, el muchacho, el niño; small —, el chico

bread, el pan

break, romper

breast, el pecho

bring, traer

broken, roto

brother, el hermano

but, pero; sino

buy, comprar

by, por; junto a, al lado de

C

call, llamar

care, el cuidado; —fully, con cuidado

carry, llevar

case, el caso; in any —, en todo caso

catch, coger; — up with, alcanzar

cause, la causa

century, el siglo

certain, cierto; seguro; a —, cierto

Charles, Carlos

chest, el pecho

child, el niño, la niña

children, los niños, los hijos

church, la iglesia; to —, a la iglesia

city, la ciudad

class, la clase; —room, la clase

clear, claro

climb, subir a

close, cerrar (ie)

coffee, el café

cold, frío, fresco; to be —, tener frío; it is —, hace frío; — water, agua fresca

color, el color

come, venir

command, mandar

commence, comenzar (ie)

companion, el compañero

company, la compañía

compel, obligar

complete, completo; —ly, por completo

condition, el estado, la condición

consider, considerar

continue, seguir (i)

contrary, contrario; on the —, al contrario

cool, fresco

count, contar (ue)

country, el país; el campo; (native) —, la tierra

course: of —, por supuesto, naturalmente

cousin, el primo, la prima

cover, cubrir

covered, cubierto

custom, la costumbre
cut, cortar

D

dare, atreverse (a)
dark, obscuro
day, el día; (two dollars) a —, (dos pesos) al día; on the following —, al día siguiente
dear, querido
death, la muerte
deceitful, traidor
deceive, engañar
December, diciembre
deep, profundo
defense, la defensa
deliver, entregar
deny, negar (ie)
depart, partir
deserve, merecer
desire, desear; el deseo
desk, la mesa
despair, desesperar
die, morir (ue)
difficult, difícil
direct, dirigir
discover, descubrir
dish, el plato
distinguish, distinguir
distress, la pena
do, hacer
dollar, el dólar, el duro, el peso
door, la puerta
doubt, dudar; la duda
down, abajo; —stairs, abajo; — the street, calle abajo
dream, el sueño; in one's —s, en sueños
dress, vestir (i), vestirse; el vestido
drink, beber

drive (a car), conducir
during, durante

E

each, cada
ear, la oreja
early, temprano
earn, ganar
earth, la tierra
easy, fácil; easily, fácilmente
eat, comer
effect, el efecto
employ, emplear
employer, el amo
end, terminar, acabar; el fin, el término
enemy, el enemigo
English, inglés
enjoy, gozar (de)
enough, bastante; to be —, bastar
enter, entrar
entire, entero
equal, igual
err, errar (ie, written ye at beginning of word)
especially, sobre todo
eternal, eterno
Europe, Europa
even, aun, hasta; — if, aunque
ever? ¿jamás? ¿alguna vez?
every, cada; — day, todos los días
evil, el mal
example, el ejemplo
except, menos
exist, existir
expect, esperar
eye, el ojo

F

face, la cara, el rostro
fact: in —, en efecto

fail, dejar de (+ *inf.*)
faith, la fe
fall, caer
family, la familia
far, lejos; **farther on, más allá**
father, el padre
favor, el favor
fear, temer; el miedo
February, febrero
feel, sentir (ie)
few, algunos, unos; pocos
field, el campo
figure, la figura
fill, llenar
find, hallar, encontrar (ue)
finger, el dedo
finish, terminar, acabar
fire, el fuego
first, primero; at —, al principio
fish, el pescado
flee, huir
floor, el suelo
flower, la flor
fly, la mosca
follow, seguir (i)
following, siguiente; **on the —** day,
    al día siguiente
foot, el pie; on —, a pie
for, para; por
forehead, la frente
forget, olvidar
form, formar; la forma
fortune, la fortuna
fountain, la fuente
Frank, Paco
free, libre
French, francés
Friday, el viernes
friend, el amigo, la amiga
from, de, desde

front: in — of, delante de
fulfill, cumplir
full, lleno

G

gain, ganar
garden, el jardín
general, general
gentleman, el caballero, el señor
German, alemán
get: — up, levantarse; — out, sacar;
    — into the (car), subir al (coche);
    — to be, llegar a ser
girl, la muchacha, la niña
give, dar
glad: be — (of) alegrarse (de)
gladly, con mucho gusto
glass, el cristal
glitter, relucir
glory, la gloria
go, ir; — away, irse; — up, subir; —
    down, bajar; — in, entrar; — out,
    salir
God, Dios
gold, el oro
good, bueno
good-by, adiós
grandfather, el abuelo
grandmother, la abuela
green, verde
grief, la pena
ground, el suelo, la tierra
guard, guardar

H

habit, la costumbre
hair, el pelo
half, medio; la mitad
hand, la mano; **on the other —, en
    cambio**

handwriting, la letra
happen, pasar, suceder
happy, feliz (*with* ser); contento (*with* estar)
hard, duro
hardly, apenas
harm, el mal
haste, la prisa
Havana, la Habana
have, tener; (*auxiliary*) haber
head, la cabeza; —ache, dolor de cabeza
health, la salud
healthy, sano
hear, oír
heart, el corazón
heat, el calor
heaven, el cielo
help, ayudar
here, aquí; here, hither, acá
history, la historia
home, la casa; at —, en casa; to go —, ir a casa
homely, feo
honor, el honor
hope, esperar; la esperanza
horse, el caballo; on —back, a caballo
hot, caliente
hour, la hora
house, la casa
how? ¿cómo?; — much, cuánto; — many, cuántos
human, humano
hunger, el hambre (*f.*)
hungry: to be —, tener hambre
hurry, la prisa; to be in a —, tener prisa
husband, el esposo, el marido

I

idea, la idea
if, si
imagine, figurarse
immediately, en seguida
impossible, imposible
in, en
indicate, indicar
industry, la industria
inside, dentro
instant, el instante
intend, pensar (ie)
interesting, interesante
introduce, presentar
island, la isla
Italian, italiano

J

January, enero
job, el trabajo; to get a —, colocarse
Joe, Pepe
John, Juan
join, unir
Joseph, José
July, julio
June, junio
justice, la justicia

K

keep, guardar, conservar
kill, matar
kind, la clase; what — of? ¿qué clase de?
king, el rey
knight, el caballero
knock, llamar a la puerta
know, saber; conocer; to — how, saber

L

lack, faltar; la falta
land, la tierra
language, la lengua, el idioma
large, grande
last, último; at —, al fin; — week, la semana pasada
late, tarde
laugh, reír; to — at, reírse de
law, la ley
lead, conducir
learn, aprender
learned, letrado
least: at —, por lo menos
leave, salir, irse; dejar; to take —, despedirse (i) de
left, izquierdo; to have —, quedarle a uno (me quedan dos)
leg, la pierna
less, menos
letter, la carta; (*of the alphabet*) la letra
liberty, la libertad
lie, la mentira
life, la vida
light, la luz
like, semejante, igual; como
lip, el labio; lower —, labio inferior; upper —, labio superior
listen, escuchar
little, pequeño; poco; a —, un poco (de)
live, vivir
lively, vivo
long, largo
look, mirar; — for, buscar
lose, perder (ie)
Louis, Luis
love, amar; querer a; el amor
low, bajo
luck, la suerte

M

mad, loco; to become —, volverse loco
madam, (la) señora
main, principal
make, hacer; — one's way toward, dirigirse a
mallet, el mazo
man, el hombre
manner, la manera
many, muchos
March, marzo
marry, casarse (con)
Mary, María
master, el amo
matter, importar; as a — of fact, en efecto; what is the — ? ¿qué pasa? what is the — with you? ¿qué tiene Vd.? ¿qué le pasa?
May, mayo
mean, querer decir
meat, la carne
meet, encontrar (ue); reunirse; conocer
memory, la memoria
mention: don't — it, de nada
merit, merecer
merry, alegre
Michael, Miguel
minute, el minuto
Miss, (la) señorita
moment, el momento
Monday, el lunes
monkey, el mono, la mona
month, el mes
more, más
morning, la mañana
most of, la mayor parte de
mother, la madre
mountain, la montaña

mourn, llorar
mouth, la boca
move, mover (ue); (*intrans.*) moverse
movement, el movimiento
Mr., (el) señor
Mrs., (la) señora
much, mucho

N

name, el nombre
natural, natural
nature, la naturaleza
near, cerca (de); junto (a)
nearly, casi
necessary, necesario, preciso
necessity, la necesidad
need, necesitar; hacer falta (I need a book, me hace falta un libro); la necesidad
neighbor, el vecino
neither, ni, tampoco; — . . . nor, ni . . . ni
never, nunca, jamás
nevertheless, sin embargo
new, nuevo
night, la noche; last —, anoche, to—, esta noche
no, no
noble, noble
nobody, nadie
none, ninguno
nor, ni; neither . . . —, ni . . . ni
nose, la nariz
nothing, nada
November, noviembre
now, ahora; ya
number, el número

O

object, el objeto
oblige, obligar

occasion, la ocasión
occupy, ocupar
October, octubre
of, de
offer, ofrecer
old, viejo, antiguo
on, en, sobre
once, una vez; at —, en seguida
only, sólo, solamente; único
open, abrir; adj., abierto
or, o; u (*before a word beginning with o or ho*); either . . . —, o . . . o
order, pedir; mandar; la orden
other, otro; the —s, los otros, los demás; —wise, de otro modo
ought, deber
outside, fuera
overtake, alcanzar
owe, deber
own, propio
owner, el dueño

P

pain, el dolor
palace, el palacio
paper, el papel
parents, los padres
part, la parte
pass, pasar
pay, pagar
peace, la paz
pen, la pluma
pencil, el lápiz
people, la gente, el pueblo
perhaps, quizá(s), tal vez
permit, permitir, dejar
person, la persona
pick up, recoger
picture, el cuadro
piece, el pedazo

place, poner, colocar; el sitio, el lugar; el puesto

plate, el plato

play (*a musical instrument*), tocar

please, gustar; haga el favor de (dármelo)

pleasure, el placer, el gusto

poet, el poeta

point, el punto

poor, pobre

Portuguese, portugués

possible, posible

poverty, la pobreza

pray, rogar (ue)

prepare, disponer; — oneself (get ready), disponerse

present, presentar; presente

preserve, conservar

pretty, bonito

pride, el orgullo

prince, el príncipe

princess, la princesa

principal, principal

produce, producir

profound, profundo

promise, la promesa; to keep (his, her, your) —, cumplir con (su) palabra

proprietor, el dueño

public, el público

pure, puro

purpose, el propósito

push aside, apartar

put, poner, colocar; — in, meter; — on, ponerse; — to bed, acostar (ue)

Q

queen, la reina

question, la pregunta; to ask a —, hacer una pregunta

quickly, pronto

R

rain, llover (ue); la lluvia

raise, levantar

rapid, rápido; —ly, rápidamente

reach, alcanzar; — one's (tenth) birthday, cumplir (diez) años

read, leer

realize, darse cuenta de

reason, la razón

receive, recibir

refer, referir (ie); to — to, referirse a

refuse to, negarse (ie) a

regard: with — to, respecto a; —s recuerdos

regret, sentir (ie)

relation, la relación; to establish business —s with, entrar en relaciones con

remain, quedar

remember, recordar (ue)

remove, quitar

repeat, repetir (i)

respect, el respeto

return, volver (ue)

rich, rico

right, derecho; to be —, tener razón

river, el río

road, el camino

room, el cuarto, la habitación; el espacio

rose, la rosa

royal, real

run, correr; (*a machine*), andar

S

sad, triste

saint, el santo, la santa

salt, la sal

same, mismo, igual

Saturday, el sábado

save, guardar, conservar

say, decir; — yes (no), decir que sí (que no)

scarcely, apenas

scene, la escena

science, la ciencia

sea, mar (*m. & f.*)

seat, sentar (ie)

seated, sentado

secret, el secreto

see, ver

seize, coger; to — by the arm, coger del brazo a

self, mismo; I my—, yo mismo

sell, vender

send, enviar, mandar

sense, el sentido

sentiment, el sentimiento

September, septiembre

serious, grave

servant, el criado, la criada

serve, servir (i)

several, varios

severe, severo

shade, la sombra; in the —, a la sombra

shoe, el zapato

short, corto, bajo; in —, en fin

show, enseñar, mostrar (ue)

sick, enfermo, malo

side, el lado

silent: to be —, callar

silk, la seda

similar, semejante

since, desde, desde que; (*causal*) puesto que

sing, cantar

sir, (el) señor

sister, la hermana

sit down, sentarse (ie)

sky, el cielo

sleep, dormir (ue); el sueño

slow, lento

small, pequeño

so, tan, así; — much, tanto; — many, tantos; — that, de modo que, de manera que

some, alguno, algunos; unos

something, algo; — else, otra cosa

son, el hijo

soon, pronto

soul, el alma (*f.*)

space, el espacio

Spain, España

Spanish, español

speak, hablar

spend (*time*), pasar

spirit, el espíritu

spite: in — of, a pesar de

spring, la primavera; la fuente

stage, la escena

stale: — bread, pan duro

start to (run), echarse a (correr)

state, el estado

stay, quedarse

step, el paso

still, todavía, aun (aún)

stone, la piedra

stop, detenerse; dejar de (+ *inf.*)

story, el cuento, la historia

street, la calle; along the —, por la calle

strength, la fuerza, las fuerzas

strong, fuerte

study, estudiar; el estudio

such, tal; — a, tal

suddenly, de pronto

suffer, sufrir

suit, el traje

summer, el verano

sun, el sol; the — is shining, hay sol

suppose, suponer

sure, seguro

sweet, dulce

T

table, la mesa

take, tomar; llevar; — off, quitarse; — out, sacar

talk, hablar

tall, alto

taste, el gusto

teach, enseñar

teacher, el maestro

tear, la lágrima

tell, decir, contar (ue)

thanks, gracias

that, que; ese, aquel; *neut.*, eso, aquello

the, el (los), la (las); *neut.*, lo

theater, el teatro

then, entonces; después, luego; pues; well —, pues entonces

there (*near one addressed*), ahí; (*yonder*) allí; — is (are), hay; — was (were), había; — will be, habrá; — would be, habría

thief, el ladrón

thing, la cosa

think, pensar (ie); creer, parecer; — about, pensar en

thirst, la sed; to be thirsty, tener sed

this, este (esta); — one, éste, ésta

thought, el pensamiento; on second —, bien considerado

through, por

throw, echar; to — into (the street), echar a (la calle)

Thursday, el jueves

thus, así

time, el tiempo; (*of day*) la hora; (*repetition*) la vez; at —s, a veces; some —s, algunas veces; from — to —, de vez en cuando; for the first —, por primera vez

tired, cansado

to, a; in order —, para

today, hoy

tomorrow, mañana

tongue, la lengua

too, también

tooth, el diente

torn, roto

touch, tocar

toward, hacia

town, el pueblo

treat, tratar

tree, el árbol

trip, el viaje

true, verdadero; it is —, es verdad; isn't it — ? ¿no es verdad? ¿verdad? ¿no?

truth, la verdad

try, tratar, procurar

Tuesday, el martes

turn, volver (ue)

U

ugly, feo

uncle, el tío; — and aunt, los tíos

under, debajo de; bajo

understand, entender (ie), comprender

unite, unir, unirse

until, hasta, hasta que

up, arriba; —stairs, arriba; — the street, calle arriba

use, usar, emplear

V

value, el valor
very, muy
view, la vista
village, el pueblo, el lugar
virtue, la virtud
voice, la voz; in a loud (low) —, en
    voz alta (baja)

W

wait, esperar
walk, andar; ir a pie
wall, la pared
war, la guerra
warm, caliente; it is —, hace calor;
    to be —, tener calor
warn, advertir (ie)
waste, perder (ie)
water, el agua (*f.*); cold —, agua
    fresca
way, el modo; by the —, a propósito
wealth, la riqueza
wear, llevar (*of clothes*)
Wednesday, el miércoles
week, la semana; last —, la semana
    pasada; next —, la semana que
    viene
weep, llorar
weigh, pesar
welcome: you are —, de nada
well, bien
what? ¿qué? ¿cuál? what a! ¡qué!
when, cuando; — ? ¿cuándo?
where, donde; — ? ¿dónde?
whether, si

which? ¿cuál?
while, mientras; el rato; in a little
    —, al poco rato
white, blanco
who, que, quien; — ? ¿quién?
whole, entero
whose, cuyo; ¿de quién?
why? ¿por qué?
wife, la esposa, la mujer
will, querer; la voluntad
wind, el viento; it is windy, hace
    viento
window, la ventana
wine, el vino
wish, querer, desear
with, con, de; — me, conmigo; —
    you (*fam.*), contigo
within, dentro de
without, sin
woman, la mujer
word, la palabra; to keep one's —,
    cumplir palabra
work, trabajar; el trabajo; la obra
world, el mundo
worth, el valor; to be —, valer
worthy, digno
write, escribir

Y

year, el año
yes, sí
yesterday, ayer
yet, todavía, aun; not —, todavía no
young, joven
youngster, el chico

Index

Numbers refer to sections.